OUR INNER BIASES

AWARENESS ALONE IS NOT ENOUGH

Dr. Zena Hamdan

Fulton Books
Meadville, PA

Published by Fulton Books 2024

ISBN 979-8-88982-311-7 (paperback)
ISBN 979-8-88982-312-4 (digital)

Printed in the United States of America

CONTENTS

CHAPTER 1

What Is Inner Bias?

Introduction
What Is "Inner Bias"?

The account presented in this book is based on the discovery of "inner bias" within the author's empirical research. The purpose of sharing the concept of "inner bias" is to uncover the theoretical and conceptual underpinnings of these findings along with describing the narratives and themes uncovered in the research. To tell this account, this author will combine the presentation of theoretical and academic literature with her own research. By presenting research in this way, the author hopes to demonstrate the foundation of the contents presented in this book within theory and extant literature while demonstrating the richness that this study offers to our existing body of knowledge.

The importance of context, including an individual's perceived background and perceived societal and cultural stereotypes, will be described regarding their impact on decision-making, both consciously and subconsciously. This importance of context that is central to the individual will be presented as the basis upon which our inner biases are formed. Within this book, we will explore how such biases are formed. With this understanding, I will present the argument that due to the intricacies and complexities upon which biases are formed, awareness of such biases alone is not enough to combat them. A discussion of the way forward based on this argument will then be discussed as well as potential "ways forward" for future research and theoretical exploration.

Outline of the Book

As noted, this book has been written to provide the reader with the underpinnings of bias and to further explore the concept of inner biases based on empirical research. This first chapter will define "Inner Bias", and will provide the reader with the theoretical literature on bias. It is an exploration of the sources of bias, as well as the impact of bias. Chapter 2 explores cultural and personal biases. Chapter 3 highlights the author research and introduces the empirical research. Chapter 4 discusses how to overcome the inner bias, the personal bias, and the cultural bias. Chapter 5 explores the bias as a human nature and provides the reader with global examples, and it includes a discussion on how one can take the first step in controlling biased perceptions.

Theories on Bias

In exploring the theories on bias, we must consider the psychological foundations for bias, the sources of bias, and the impact of bias. Each of these factors is key to exploring and understanding the formation of our inner biases. We will begin by exploring the psychological foundations for bias. As will be described, the theories on bias are rooted in cognitive psychology.

Psychological Foundations for Bias

Although bias is also based within sociology, bias will be presented here, first, in terms of its psychological foundation, which is based in cognitive psychology. Cognitive psychology provides a means of understanding individual perceptions and the formation of memory, thinking, and information processing. Within this understanding, there is a connection between the thinking mind and the physical mind. In this relationship, the physical mind is responsible for the neurophysiological activities that correspond with the memory, thinking, and information processing that occurs within the thinking mind.[1]

This connection is the process by which human cognition takes place and allows for sensation, perception, attention, memory, and higher-order cognition.[2] Within these complex dynamics, consciousness, language, and problem-solving also occur, which includes reactions and interactions between the individual and other beings.[3] With the psychological foundations for bias established, in the section to follow, we will explore cognitive bias.

Cognitive bias

Cognitive biases are how our mind makes quick decisions. In some views, cognitive biases help to improve our efficiency by allowing us to make such decisions quickly. However, decisions made quickly based on cognitive bias do not involve the process of conscious deliberation. This then leads us to the question: if not conscious deliberation, what are the decisions made based on? The answer to this question is connected to the concept of bias. Cognitive biases are based on the concept of *subjective reality*.

As mentioned previously, human cognition is the basis upon which individuals process information and allows for sensation, per-

---

[1] Solso, M. K. MacLin, and O. H. MacLin, *Cognitive Psychology*.

[2] Ibid.

[3] Hart, "Adaptive Heuristics," 1401–1430; Kahneman, Slovic, and Tversky, *Judgment Under Uncertainty: Heuristics and Biases*.

ception, attention, and memory. Cognition includes motivational, affective, and behavioral processes.[4] Therefore, cognitive biases, which are based on an individual's subjective reality, impact the decision-making process, which is based on their subjective reality and judgment. Although cognitive bias allows for quick decision-making, the consequences of relying on cognitive bias include poor decision-making and judgment due to the lack of conscious deliberation. Understanding the underlying influences on cognitive bias is important in understanding the factors that impact the decisions and judgments of individuals, particularly in instances in which reflection and deliberation are not involved.

Heuristics

Heuristics refers to the process by which an individual makes quickly formed decisions or judgments or finds a solution to an identified issue. Specifically, heuristics is associated with the strategies used to frame decision tasks. Heuristics, in general, has been used in basic terms to refer to simple behaviors.[5] In this way, in this book, heuristics is a central concept to bias as our quickly formed decisions and judgments are often based on or at least influenced by our biases. We will return to this connection between cognitive bias and heuristics in the next section, after first exploring the applications of adaptive heuristics in complex decision-making.

Although it is important to explore the implications for heuristics on the thoughts and behaviors of individuals, we must keep in mind the context of the applicability of heuristics in understanding human behavior. As we are aware, both in literature and in exposure to the behaviors of others, the behaviors of individuals tend to be complex. Further to the concept of heuristics as guiding the quickly formed decisions of individuals, *adaptive heuristics* refers to the rules of behavior. In exploring the rules of behavior, Hart (2005)

---

4   Schwarz, "Social Judgment and Attitudes: Warmer, More Social, and Less Conscious," 149–176.

5   Hart, "Adaptive Heuristics," 1401–1430.

presented that we are bounded by rational strategies but "bounded away" from full rationality. Adaptive heuristics is therefore key in understanding behavior within dynamic settings. Adaptive heuristics has been applied in behavior models to follow the behaviors of individuals, particularly when it appears that individuals are making "better" decisions.[6]

Heuristics and Biases

With the overview of heuristics and cognitive biases presented separately, we now return to the connection between them. Daniel Kahneman, a psychologist and economist, has explored the relationships between cognitive biases and heuristics as related to decision-making, judgment, and human rationality more broadly. In *Judgment Under Uncertainty: Heuristics and Biases*, Kahneman, Slovic, and Tversky (1982) address the three aspects of heuristics:

a. Availability (of instances or scenarios)
b. Representativeness (based on instances in which individuals are asked to judge the probability that an object or event belongs to a certain class or process)
c. Anchoring and adjustment[7]

The purpose of exploring these three aspects of heuristics is to link heuristics to judgment—particularly in instances in which decisions are made in situations in which conditions are uncertain. For example, representativeness judgment, according to Tversky and Kahneman, can be explored using the following four cases as examples:

---

[6] Ibid.

[7] Kahneman, Slovic, and Tversky, *Judgment Under Uncertainty: Heuristics and Biases.*

1. M is a class, and X is a value of a variable defined in this class.
2. M is a class, and X is an instance of that class.
3. M is a class, and X is a subset of M.
4. M is a (causal) system, and X is a (possible) consequence.[8]

In following the argument for judgment as related to heuristics, following Kahneman and colleagues, our decisions are based on the availability of information, perception of risk, and previous experiences. However, as expressed by Kahneman, Slovic, and Tversky (1982), this perception may be "incorrect" as it is based on heuristics—the way in which we quickly make decisions:

> Many decisions are based on beliefs concerning the likelihood of uncertain events such as the outcome of an election, the guilt of a defendant, or the future value of the dollar... What determines such beliefs? How do people assess the probability of an uncertain event or the value of an uncertain quantity?... People rely on a limited number of heuristic principles which reduce the complex tasks of assessing probabilities and predicting values to simpler judgmental operations. In general, these heuristics are quite useful, but sometimes they lead to severe and systematic errors.[9]

Although Kahneman et al. (1982) focus on the biases that are produced based on judgmental heuristics, here we argue that the inverse is true. Because heuristics is formed by our biases, our judgment not only produces bias but is also influenced by our own cognitive biases. Understanding this relationship helps to understand why humans seem to diverge from reasoning based on their intu-

---

8   Ibid.
9   Ibid., 3.

ition. The reason for this divergence is based on heuristics and biases. Below, we further explore judgment and decision-making to deepen the connection between heuristics and biases with judgment and decision-making.

Judgment and decision-making

Judgment and decision-making have their basis in not only psychology but also in the disciplines of economics, philosophy, and management science.[10] As a field, judgment and decision-making is normative, descriptive, and prescriptive.[11] The science of judgment and decision-making involves the analysis of the decisions experienced by individuals, the natural responses to these decisions, and the interventions that can be used to help individuals make better decisions.[12] In other words, following Fischhoff (2010), these three aspects of judgment and decision-making can be understood as follows:

- *normative analysis* identify the best courses of action, given decision-makers' values;
- *descriptive studies* examine actual behavior in terms comparable to the normative analyses; and
- *prescriptive interventions* help individuals to make better choices. Prescriptive interventions bridge the gap between the normative ideal and the descriptive reality.[13]

Judgment and decision-making allows for us to evaluate judgments and decisions as "better or worse" with the potential to intro-

---

[10] Fischhoff, "Judgment and Decision Making," 724–735.

[11] Fischhoff, "Judgment and Decision Making," 724–735; Baron, "Normative Models of Judgment and Decision Making," 19–36; Freeling, "A Philosophical Basis for Decision Aiding," 179–206; Baron, *Rationality and Intelligence*; Bell, Raiffa, and Tversky, *Decision Making: Descriptive, Normative, and Prescriptive Interactions.*

[12] Fischoff and Broomell, "Judgment and Decision Making," 331–355.

[13] Fischhoff, "Judgement and Decision Making," 724–735.

duce interventions to improve them.[14] As related to decision-making, judgment involves the process by which individuals make decisions by predicting what might happen based on the different choices or options available. In the process of prediction, Fischoff and Broomell (2020) highlight the importance of individuals' beliefs as impacting the accuracy and consistency of their judgment:

> The quality of those judgments can be evaluated in terms of their accuracy or their consistency. Studies of both accuracy and consistency build on analytical research formalizing these criteria. Achieving one goal need not mean achieving the other. People may have accurate beliefs about one topic but not about related ones, leading to inconsistent judgments; or they may have consistent beliefs but know very little. Both criteria continue to be central topics in behavioral decision research, or decision science, as the field is sometimes called.[15]

The purpose of judgment and decision-making is to compare the judgments to standards. By comparing judgments to standards, judgment and decision-making, the purpose is to evaluate whether judgments are better or worse. Judgments, in turn, involve decisions, in which individuals make judgments about what to do.[16] Another key point related to judgment and beliefs is consistency. Individuals are able to evaluate and change or "update" their beliefs. The standard of consistency in judgment is Bayesian inference, which establishes the rules by which individuals evaluate evidence and update their beliefs.[17]

---

14 Baron, "The Point of Normative Models in Judgment and Decision Making," 577.

15 Fischoff and Broomell, "Judgment and Decision Making," 333.

16 Baron, "Normative Models of Judgment and Decision Making," 19–36.

17 Fischoff and Broomell, "Judgment and Decision Making," 331–355; Edwards, Lindman, and Savage, "Bayesian Statistical Inference for Psychological

Normative models

As noted above, normative models focus on the values of the individual decision-makers that influence their decisions.[18] Normative models are named as such because they are norms. According to Baron, "Normative models must be understood in terms of their role in looking for biases, understanding these biases in terms of descriptive models, and developing prescriptive models."[19]

The standards for normative models, which can be used to evaluate judgment and decision-making are primarily based on probability theory, utility theory, and statistics. From these fields, mathematic theories or models are used to help evaluate judgment, including decisions.[20] To illustrate normative models in judgment and decision-making, we present the examples of normative models presented by Baron (2012):

1. For quantitative judgments (e.g., populations of cities, proportions of coin tosses that were heads), the normative model is simply the right answers. This also applies to relative judgments (which city has more people?) or judgments of category membership. We can also quantify departures from the right answers in various ways.

2. For judgments of the probability of unique events, one type of normative model, which is applied to a group of such judgments, scores the judgments by distance from 0 (no) to 1 (yes) and applies some formula to these scores. A related approach is to aggregate judgments with the same stated probability (e.g., all those with 80 percent) and ask if the proportion is correct (calibration, the proposition should be true 80 percent of the time).

Research," 193–242; Kyburg and Smokler, *Studies in Subjective Probability.*

[18] Fischoff and Broomell, "Judgment and Decision Making," 331–355.

[19] Baron, "Normative Models of Judgment and Decision Making," 19–36; Baron, *Rationality and Intelligence.*

[20] Baron, "Normative Models of Judgment and Decision Making," 19–36.

3. Alternatively, for probabilities of related unique events, we can assess their coherence, their agreement with each other. If you say that the probability is 0.6 that X will win a competition and 0.7 that Y will win, you are not coherent.
4. For decisions, we can sometimes assess their consistency with basic principles of decision-making, such as dominance (if A is better than B in some respects and worse in no respects, then choose A).
5. More typically, we assess the coherence of sets of decisions using a mathematical model to define coherence. *Utility* is a summary measure of *good(ness)*.[21]

Social judgment theory

With the exploration of the complexities between judgment, bias, and decision-making, we now present social judgment theory. Social judgment theory is founded in judgment theory and was developed by psychologist Muzafer Sherif along with Carl I. Hovland and Carolyn W. Sherif. Sherif et al. (1965) described attitudes as "the stands the individual upholds and cherishes about objects, issues, persons, groups, or institutions."[22] The importance of social judgment theory is that it posits the notion that the attitudes formed by the individual are cognitively based. Moreover, social context and cultural influences impact social judgment, which thereby impacts the judgment of the individual on a cognitive level.[23] Due to the multiple influences involved, an individual's attitudes are complex and based on a range of attitudes.

---

[21] Baron, "The Point of Normative Models in Judgment and Decision Making," 577.

[22] M. Sherif, C. Sherif, and Nebergall, *Attitude and Attitude Change: The Social Judgment-Involvement Approach*, 4.

[23] Schwarz, "Social Judgment and Attitudes: Warmer, More Social, and Less Conscious," 149–176.

Connecting Judgment, Bias, and Decision-Making

We close this section to draw the connections between judgment, bias, and decision-making. As demonstrated in the previous section, bias influences decision-making because bias impacts the judgments individuals form. In turn, the judgments formed by individuals are used to make decisions, which are thereby based on their biases. Judgments are also based on previous decision-making as the consequences of an individual's previous actions and behaviors (in the form of decisions) are used to inform future decision-making. With the importance of bias in the link between decision-making and judgment, we now turn to the sources of bias.

Sources of Bias—the Formation of Our Inner Biases

The sources of bias are based both on the individual and collective level. Together, our inner biases are formed based on cultural biases and personal biases. Because we as individuals are socialized, many of our personal biases are based on influences from the collective level and may therefore be reflective of the cultural biases that we are exposed to on the collective level. This dynamic will be further described, beginning with the concept of cultural bias, which exists at the collective level.

Cultural bias

The concept of cultural bias is central to this book as it influences the variance in bias on a collective level. "Culture shapes how we perceive ourselves and interact with the world. It is the lens through which we organize our reasoning and our emotional response."[24] Of

---

[24] Kirmayer, Rousseau, and Lashley, "The Place of Culture in Forensic Psychiatry," 98; Friedman, "Culture, Bias, and Understanding: We Can Do Better," 166–139.

importance to understanding cultural bias is the impact of cultural bias on establishing differences between groups. This difference is made by the individual based on these learned distinctions, which are based on cultural bias. Cultural biases are established or internalized into inner biases at an early age as children are socialized and adopt the biases of their society and culture. As expressed by Yingst (2011), who explored cultural bias within child behavior and development, cultural bias is closely related to judgment, particularly in prejudice:

> Cultural bias involves a prejudice or highlighted distinction in viewpoint that suggests a preference of one culture over another. Cultural bias can be described as discriminative. There is a lack of group integration of social values, beliefs, and rules of conduct. Cultural bias introduces one group's accepted behavior as valued and distinguishable from another lesser valued societal group.[25]

In addition to the variation in individual bias, which exists on a cognitive level, it is important to note that the cultural bias of individuals is influenced by their complex sociocultural context. Cultural bias, therefore, creates differences between groups based on cultural differences.

Cultural bias adds to the complexity of the individual-level bias that is innate in each individual. To understand cultural bias, one must consider the differences both among and between groups and individuals:

> Cultural bias highlights differences among persons and groups. Cultural bias groupings can be identified in differential characteristic preferences. They may include differences in levels of socio-economic status, language, race, ethnicity,

---

[25] Yingst, "Cultural Bias."

religion, or sexuality. Cultural bias can support myths or stereotypes of cultures and in similar fashion may lead to racial and ethnic profiling.[26]

Although cultural bias is a key consideration in understanding judgment and decision-making, we must highlight the difference between cultural bias and cultural relativity. Cultural relativity is separate from cultural bias in that cultural relativism is based on understanding an individual's beliefs, values, and practices based on the norms of their own culture. In contrast, cultural bias involves the judgments and preconceptions that an individual has based on the norms within their own culture. Cultural relativism, however, is required for understanding how cultural bias may be formed. Moreover, cultural bias is developed within the process of socialization:

> Cultural bias is learned and develops as the child understands and functions comfortably within an immediate group (society). By the age of 5, children are aware of their cultural and ethnic background as well as the differences between themselves and others. These differences and how they are introduced to the child set the stage for cultural bias may be observed in their speech and behavior toward those who are different. Bias is introduced in how the child has been taught to value or de-value the identified cultural difference.[27]

Social norms, which are founded within the culture and society in which they are socialized impact their behaviors and decision-making. The reason for this impact is due to the bias related to sociocultural norms. Cultural bias may be influenced by interests,

---

[26] Ibid.

[27] Ibid.

but it is not easily corrected as they are based on culture and society rather than within the individual.[28]

Personal bias

Impartiality, particularly from the human account, is impossible. Personal bias, which is based on our interpretations and judgments, is unavoidable. Moreover, these biases are often difficult to distinguish from cultural bias and cultural relativity.[29] Personal bias is important as it directly impacts an individual's judgment and decision-making. Personal bias is formed both by personal values, beliefs, and those influenced by societal and cultural bias.

The Impact of Bias—the Role of Inner Bias

In this chapter, we have provided the theoretical and conceptual groundings for understanding, bias, decision-making, and judgment. We have demonstrated that bias, which, in turn, impacts judgment and decision-making, includes both the individual cognitive and personal biases of the individual and the cultural bias that influences these biases. Whether cognitive, personal (conscious), or cultural, these intertwined biases form our *inner bias*. Together, this inner bias impacts our judgment and decision-making. Here, we conclude by reviewing the impact of bias and the role of inner bias on three key areas: (a) decision-making, (b) intuitive judgment, and (c) critical thinking.

---

[28] Yingst, "Cultural Bias"; Friedman, "Culture, Bias, and Understanding: We Can Do Better," 166–139; Hebl, and Dovidio, "Promoting the 'Social' in the Examination of Social Stigmas," 156–182.

[29] Mccullagh, "Bias in Historical Description, Interpretation, and Explanation," 39–66.

Decision-making

In reflecting on the concepts presented in this chapter, it is important to keep in mind that decision-making is based on judgments about the decisions and individuals is presented. Decision-making is influenced by judgment, which is impacted by bias. The foundation between decision, judgment, and bias has been made. To further demonstrate this point, we highlight a note made by Mega et al. (2015) to connect the concept of cognitive processes and intuitive judgment:

> The intuitive decision maker is not aware of the ongoing cognitive processes, in the sense that she can report on them—neither on the cue(s) she is using (i.e., recognition) nor on the way in which the cue(s) are processed—she is, however, aware of a feeling indicating which option to choose or which action to pursue. This consciously experienced (subjective/gut) feeling is suggested to result from the ongoing cognitive processes and signifies intuitive judgments.[30]

Intuitive judgment

Intuitive judgment, in simple terms, is the decision made by an individual based on a subjective feeling or "intuition." An important note to be made is that there is a lack of consensus among researchers on the definition of intuition. Volz and Zander (2014) pointed out the issue in the lack of specific definition:

> A "condensed definition" has been put forward emphasizing that intuition is based on auto-

---

[30] Mega, Gigerenzer, and Volz, "Do Intuitive and Deliberate Judgments Rely on Two Distinct Neural Systems? A Case Study in Face Processing"; Volz, and Zander, "Primed for Intuition?" 26–34.

matic processes that rely on knowledge structures acquired through different kinds of learning. This definition further posits that intuitions operate at least partially without a person's awareness but nevertheless result in feelings, signals, or interpretations. In short, intuition is a non-conscious process exerting influence on behavior by drawing on implicitly acquired knowledge that signals higher processing areas in the conscious brain. Such a minimal definition of intuition resembles the generally accepted definition of implicit memory, at least as it appears in priming, which is itself understood as "a change in the ability to identify, produce, or classify an item as a result of a previous encounter with that item or a related item." This superficial similarity, however, raises the fundamental question of whether the concepts of intuition and implicit memory, as it functions in priming, do in fact differ, and whether this comparison could yield a clear and precise definition of intuition.[31]

Despite the lack of a defined definition, researchers have highlighted that intuitive judgment may not be fully conscious.[32] Specifically, in exploring the difference between intuitive and deliberative judgment, note that "intuitive judgments are assumed to be quick, associative, not conscious, effortless, heuristic, and—by some—error prone."[33] Intuitive judgment is based on cognitive bias

---

[31] Volz, and Zander, "Primed for Intuition?" 26–34.

[32] Mega, Gigerenzer, and Volz, "Do Intuitive and Deliberate Judgments Rely on Two Distinct Neural Systems? A Case Study in Face Processing"; Volz, and Zander, "Primed for intuition?" 26–34.

[33] Mega, Gigerenzer, and Volz, "Do Intuitive and Deliberate Judgments Rely on Two Distinct Neural Systems? A Case Study in Face Processing."

and is both subjective and based on the multiple biases that influence an individual's cognition.[34]

Critical thinking

The issue of evaluating evidence independent of one's own biases is a key aspect of critical thinking as individuals tend to be biased by prior thinking and beliefs. However, "virtually all measures of critical thinking try to assess the ability to avoid reasoning that is too biased by prior opinion and prior belief (e.g., Ennis, Millman, and Tomko, 1985; Facione, 1992; Norris and Ennis, 1989; Watson and Glaser, 1980)."[35]

Critical thinking itself is the process by which individuals form a judgment based on the information they receive. The critical thinking process is complex and involves the analysis of factual information. Although the analysis of factual information in critical thinking should be unbiased and based on the evidence, the process itself is often biased.[36] The process of critical thinking is self-directed, self-disciplined, and self-monitored and is therefore subjective to the individual.[37]

---

[34] VandenBos, "Intuitive Judgment"; Mega, Gigerenzer, and Volz, "Do Intuitive and Deliberate Judgments Rely on Two Distinct Neural Systems? A Case Study in Face Processing."

[35] West, Stanovich, and Toplak, "Heuristics and Biases as Measures of Critical Thinking: Associations with Cognitive Ability and Thinking Dispositions," 930–941.

[36] West, Stanovich, and Toplak, "Heuristics and Biases as Measures of Critical Thinking: Associations with Cognitive Ability and Thinking Dispositions," 930–941; Ennis, *Critical Thinking*; Ennis, Millman, and Tomko, *Cornell Critical Thinking Tests*; Facione, *California Critical Thinking Skills Test & California Critical Thinking Dispositions Inventory*; Facione, *Critical Thinking: What It Is and Why It Counts*; Norris and Ennis, *Evaluating Critical Thinking*; Watson and Glaser, *Watson-Glaser Critical Thinking Appraisal*.

[37] Clarke, *Critical Dialogues: Thinking Together in Turbulent Times*.

Summary

Decision-making and judgment are impacted by bias because they are influenced by bias. An individual's process of decision-making involves judgment about which decisions to make and the consequences of those decisions. In the case of cognitive bias, individuals often make decisions quickly based on such biases, which are influenced by both cultural and personal biases. With this concept established, we now turn to further explore our inner biases. In chapter 2, we will explain what has been yet to be explored in the literature to provide the context for the empirical study to be presented in this book.

CHAPTER 2

Cultural and Personal Biases

Introduction
Exploring Cultural and Personal Biases

Chapter 1 provided an overview of the concepts and theoretical framing for biases, including an explanation of the formation of our inner biases. As presented, cultural and personal bias are key sources of the formation of our inner bias. In this chapter, I will provide an overview of factors pertaining to cultural and personal biases, with an emphasis on illustrative cases. An exploration of cultural and personal bias will provide a foundation for the presentation of empirical cases I have encountered in exploring our "inner bias." Before presenting empirical cases, illustrative cases will be introduced to explore the role of cultural and personal biases.

Illustrative Case Explorations

To provide a realistic exploration of cultural and personal biases, particularly concerning judgment and decision-making, I will present conflict case studies presented by Erbe (2019)[38] and examples of bias within health-care practice, as presented by Haddad et al. (2019).[39] The cases presented by Erbe (2019) have been field-tested and designed to provide individuals with an exploration of real-life scenarios,[40] thereby providing realistic explorations relevant for exploring judgment and decision-making. The cases presented by Erbe (2019) have also been selected as decision-making surrounding conflict is tangible—it involves the understanding of the factors that guide the decisions and judgment associated with one's response to conflict. Similarly, understanding the role of bias within health-care practice as explored by Haddad et al. (2019) demonstrates the significance bias has on our actions and behaviors. The cases from Haddad et al. (2019) are also significant as they demonstrate the impact that bias has on others subjected to the actions and behaviors we take based on our biases.

By understanding the factors that pertain to an individual's response to conflict and the role of bias in health-care practice, we can better understand how actions are influenced by inner biases. I present inner biases as being influenced by cultural and personal biases, which will be further explored in this chapter. We first turn to cultural bias as a bias on the collective level.

---

[38] Erbe, *Conflict Case Studies*.

[39] Haddad, Doherty, and Purtilo, "Chapter 5—Respect in a Diverse Society."

[40] According to Erbe (2019):

These case studies have been field-tested with many different groups, ages eighteen to sixty, representing diverse groups within and outside the United States, and a wide range of interests, disciplines and professions. They include peace and conflict studies, social welfare, various sciences, public health and policy, psychology, pre-medicine, nursing, law, environmental and development studies, engineering, ethnic and area studies, education, communications, business and political science. The issues raised in these cases are relevant and meaningful to most, partially because the detail provided is only what is essential to introduce the issues for exploration.

Cultural Bias

As presented in chapter 1, cultural bias is a bias that occurs at the collective level. Cultural bias influences our inner biases within the process of socialization. As a reminder, I have presented the following definition as a means to understand cultural bias: "Culture shapes how we perceive ourselves and interact with the world. It is the lens through which we organize our reasoning and our emotional response."[41] Cultural bias is key to the formation of our inner biases because it shapes our understanding of difference at the social level.

Because cultural bias establishes differences between groups based on differences in culture, cultural bias forms our inner biases as it shapes our understanding of our belonging to a group. As a member of a particular cultural group, we establish our inner biases by distinguishing ourselves from others. Those that are considered to be others are those that are different from us, based on our cultural belonging. In other words, cultural bias formulates our inner biases by shaping who we consider different from ourselves based on their belonging to a different cultural group from our own.

Although this concept appears basic and is accepted within the psychology and social sciences, the practical implications for cultural bias need to be explored a bit further. What I have left only loosely answered to this point is: *What should be considered culture?* In answering this question, we use the following definition:

> Culture is defined as the meanings and values that arise amongst distinctive social groups and classes, on the basis of their historical conditions and relationships, through which they handle and respond to the conditions of existence. It is also defined as the lived traditions and practices through which those "understandings"

---

[41] Kirmayer, Rousseau, and Lashley, "The Place of Culture in Forensic Psychiatry," 98; Friedman, "Culture, Bias, and Understanding: We Can Do Better," 166–139.

> are expressed and in which they are embodied. In almost every society, people, in their day-to-day experiences and through meeting different people, interact with several cultures. Thus, identity is determined by multiple cultures and has varied contents—every person is in a sense multicultural.[42]

In defining culture and multifaceted and considering each individual to be multicultural, we demonstrate the formation of the cultural bias aspect of our inner bias originates from multiple sources potentially indistinguishable from one another. As cultural bias shapes our own judgments and decision-making, I proposed here that cultural bias influences our inner bias not only in the formation of judgments such as prejudice[43] but also plays a role in our decisions and therefore actions. This is consistent with the definition for culture presented above, which reflects the importance of culture for shaping both the identity and the day-to-day experiences, traditions, and practices of individuals.

In addition to establishing collective differences based on characteristics such as socioeconomic status, language, race, ethnicity, religion, sexuality,[44] we also differentiate ourselves based on our cultural practices. More than establishing differentiation from others and separating ourselves from "other" cultural groups based on this sense of belonging, our culture shapes our actions, thoughts, and expressions, as demonstrated by the influence of culture on our traditions and practices. Culture not only plays a role in developing cultural bias but also influences our behaviors and culture, and in turn, cultural bias forms our cognition.

The importance of this point is in the understanding that our inner biases are not only the differences we create between ourselves and other groups but also the cognitive biases that are influenced

---

[42] Sagiv, "Cultural Bias in Judicial Decision Making," 35.
[43] Yingst, "Cultural Bias."
[44] Ibid.

by cultural bias. I proposed that cultural relativism, which is based on our understandings of the beliefs, values, practices, and norms based on our belongingness to a particular group, in turn, shapes our actions. As evidence of this point, I turn again to the basis of cultural relatives as related to our practices and norms. Based on our understanding of practices and norms, as individuals, we engage in behaviors that we believe to be acceptable based on our understanding of our culture.

Although there is the presumption that we, as rational human beings, have autonomy over our decisions and actions, the role of cultural bias cannot be overlooked. I again emphasize the fact that cultural bias may be influenced by interests, but it is not easily corrected as they are based on culture and society rather than within the individual.[45] Although cultural bias is based on culture and society rather than the individual, the influence of such bias on the actions of the individual is maintained as it is interwoven within the inner bias and therefore the development of cognitive bias within the individual. Further to this point, the role of cultural bias is expressed by Haddad et al. (2019) in the context of health care as follows:

> A cultural bias is a tendency to interpret a word or action according to culturally derived meaning assigned to it. Cultural bias derives from cultural variation…For example, some cultures view smiles as a deeply personal sign of happiness that is only shared with intimates. Others view smiles as an indication of general friendliness to be shared with all. It is quite possible that another can interpret a friendly smile on the part of one person as disingenuous or inappropriate. Regarding health care, attitudes toward pain, methods of conveyance of bad news, management

---

[45] Yingst, "Cultural Bias"; Friedman, "Culture, Bias, and Understanding: We Can Do Better," 166–139; Hebl and Dovidio, "Promoting the 'Social' in the Examination of Social Stigmas," 156–182.

of chronic illness and disability, beliefs about the seriousness and causes of illness, and death-related issues vary among different cultures.[46]

We expand on the importance of cultural bias by presenting an exploratory case by Erbe (2019) and presenting the implications for cultural bias in health care as expressed by Haddad et al. (2019) in the next sections.

Cultural Bias Case Exploration

Introduction: cultural bias exploratory case study

The case study relevant to cultural bias as presented by Erbe (2019) is "Cultural Competence: Ethical and Empowered Response with Discrimination."[47] To provide framing for this case, Erbe (2019) presented the following:

> With cultural issues, majority and minority are used to avoid the stereotyping that unfortunately still too often accompanies specific labels. The open-ended cases allow readers to introduce, discuss and show their own cultural expectations and preferences with each other... Everyone attempts to identify, describe and explain their own cultural experience, assumptions, values and preferences as they participate in conflict resolution experience. Ideally, the result is truly inclusive. At least, participants are empowered. The ideal response is like one elicited with a Hmong student. One of the case studies resonated with her experience in the United States as a first-gen-

---

[46] Haddad, Doherty, and Purtilo, "Chapter 5—Respect in a Diverse Society."
[47] Erbe, *Conflict Case Studies.*

eration immigrant and the first member of her family to feel comfortable speaking English. As a result, she spoke in great detail about her family's many cultural challenges and conflicts. Readers are invited to reference and consider their own life experience with conflict whenever analyzing and discussing case studies.

Like the Hmong student and her experiences as an immigrant in the United States, each individual has their own cultural bias and experiences the cultural biases of others. Based on the guidance presented by Erbe (2019), I present the power balancing and gender parts of "Cultural Competence: Ethical and Empowered Response with Discrimination"[48] and urge the reader to reflect upon their own experiences, inviting others to participate in this case study. As cultural bias is collective, the exploration of the case is most effective with the involvement of multiple individuals. In the section following the case study, I will reflect upon the case and present implications.

Case study: "Cultural Competence: Ethical and Empowered Response with Discrimination"[49]

Instructions: When one negotiator speaks, others laugh, look down and away, interrupt, and eat.

Questions:

1. How does intimidation look? Sound? Feel?
2. Do your assumptions and analysis change if all negotiators are men? Women? One man negotiating with a group of women?
3. You are asked to offer ideas for improving negotiations. How would you first check out all perspectives?

---

[48] Ibid.

[49] Erbe, *Conflict Case Studies*.

Cultural exploration: Gender messages

Instructions: List three messages you heard or saw as a child for each of the following categories.

Boys and girls:

   1.
   2.
   3.

Question: What did your parents and other important adults show you?

Women and men:

   1.
   2.
   3.

Question: What messages did you receive outside of your home—from television, movies, schools?

Great, strong, popular, successful…men/boys and girls/women:

   1.
   2.
   3.

Question: When did you receive the most attention (positive and negative) as a child?

Instructions: List messages and examples of ways women and men communicate, problem-solve, and resolve conflict.

Men:
Women:

Research compares "male communication" and "male communication culture" with "female communication" and "female communication culture."[50]

Suggested: When reading the following, notice where you agree and disagree.

Women	Men
Talk to build and keep rapport	Talk to assert self and ideas
Share self and learn through disclosure	Do not share self and feel vulnerable through disclosure
Talk to create equality	Talk to create status and power
Match experience with others	Match experiences to compete and show understanding and empathy and command attention: "I can top that"

---

[50] Wood, *Gender, Communication and Culture, Intercultural Communication;* see also Wall and Dewhurst, *Mediator Gender: Communication Differences in Resolved and Unresolved Mediations;* Weingarten and Douvan, "Male and Female Visions of Mediation," 349–358.

Support others by expressing	Support others by doing something understanding of feelings and being helpful, like giving advice or solving problem for another
Include others in conversation	Do not "share the stage" with others by asking for opinions and interrupting to make points and being unencouraging and not waiting for their turn to speak
Keeps the conversation going by asking	Assert self and ideas, questions and show interest
Listen empathetically and actively	Build ideas competitively
Are tentative so others feel free	Are assertive so seen as confident and add in command

Cultural exploration

Instructions: Observe men and women communicating. Notice who talks most and the following:

Question: Are "traditional" men more

- aggressive?
- directive?
- controlling?
- dominating?
- goal-oriented?

Question: Do "traditional" men use more

- hostile language (e.g., profane, sexual, etc.)?
- suggestions and opinions?

Question: Do "traditional" women

- qualify their language?
- hedge?

Question: Do "traditional" women use more

- disclaimers?
- questions at the end of their statements?
- verbal "fillers"/extras?
- laugh more?

Question: Are "traditional" women more

- indirect?
- supportive?
- giving of more information?

Cultural exploration: Conflict resolution preferences

Question: What best describes your ideals? Try creating your own.

1. I am expected to get the "best deal possible."
2. I am "my own person." I like people who know their own potential and work to maximize.
3. How you get there is as, perhaps more, important than the end: peace by peaceful means.
4. I believe there are certain problems that should be solved by men.
5. I am confused about modern male-female relationships and rules.

6. Women and children should not be publicly involved.
7. No one owes anyone anything.
8. "Survival of the fittest" or "every man for himself."
9. Survival is the rule when you are poor.
10. The end justifies the means.
11. Some degree of compromise may be necessary with conflict.
12. People should help themselves. Enabling weakens.

Instructions: Discuss the implications for your views on the questions above.

Reflection on cultural bias exploratory case study

In exploring cultural bias within this case study, we can see from the exploration of the case that cultural bias shapes our behaviors and is based on societal norms. Additionally, cultural bias on the societal level fuels issues of discrimination and inequity. The example provided demonstrates cultural bias on the level, particularly of power and gender norms. In the next section, we will explore the practical considerations of cultural bias in health care.

Cultural Bias Implications

Referring to the case of cultural bias in health care, we turn to Haddad et al. (2019), who stated the following:

> Management of chronic illness and disability, beliefs about the seriousness and causes of illness, and death-related issues vary among different cultures. These different kinds of beliefs about disease and illness have an impact on health care–seeking behavior and acceptance of the advice, status, and intervention of health professionals. Understanding a patient's concept of health and illness is critical to the development

> of interaction strategies that are clinically sound
> and acceptable to the patient.[51]

As evident by this statement, the implications for cultural bias as demonstrated in the case of interactions in health care are that cultural biases shape the views of individuals, including their communication and expectation within social interactions. In this example, we see that cultural bias, therefore, shapes bias on the individual level. We will further explore the concept of personal bias as intertwined with cultural bias and implications for cognition.

Personal Bias

As presented in chapter 1, personal bias is embedded with our interpretations and judgments as human beings. The formation of human judgment and decision-making is, in turn, based on these personal biases.[52] Just as personal bias and impartiality are impossible, bias within judgments and interpretations are, therefore, unavoidable. Here, we explore further the complex formation of personal bias based on personal values, beliefs, and the societal and cultural bias presented in the prior section. The importance of exploring personal bias in addition to cultural bias and cultural relatively is to demonstrate the difficulty, in some cases, separating the personal biases formed by the individual.[53]

Personal bias, as it is based on the individual level, although influenced by cultural bias based in society and culture, is formed based on an individual's personal experience:

> A personal bias is a tendency to interpret a
> word or action in terms of a personal significance

---

[51] Haddad, Doherty, and Purtilo, "Chapter 5—Respect in a Diverse Society."

[52] Kerr, MacCoun, and Kramer, "Bias in Judgment: Comparing Individuals and Groups," 687.

[53] Mccullagh, "Bias in Historical Description, Interpretation, and Explanation," 39–66.

assigned to it. Personal bias can derive from culturally defined interpretations but also can originate from other sources grounded in personal experience. The individual internalizes the cultural attitudes until he or she believes them to be entirely personal. Put another way, a personal bias is an individual's feeling about a particular person or thing that colors his or her interpretation of it. The bias can lead to more favorable or less favorable judgments than are warranted.[54]

Like the lack of collective understanding or cultural bias, individuals tend not to recognize their own personal biases.[55] However, as expressed in the statement presented by Haddad et al. (2019), personal bias shapes our judgment and, in some cases, leads to the differential and even negative response to situations and treatment of other individuals based on our internalized personal bias. Personal bias, in other words, like the internalization of societal and cultural values within collective bias, is internalized[56] and impacts our cognitive bias.

Although the complexities of personal bias and cultural bias have been explored in empirical research and the subject of theorizing by scholars, there has been a lack of in-depth exploration of how they comprehensively form our inner biases. As we will see in the case studies, the exploration of persona bias has been largely limited to the role of personal bias in shaping our actions toward others rather than a broader exploration of the influence of personal bias on our cognition. We will return to this point and implications for further exploration in this book in chapter 3.

---

[54] Haddad, Doherty, and Purtilo, "Chapter 5—Respect in a Diverse Society."
[55] Ibid.
[56] Ibid.

Personal Bias Case Exploration

Personal bias may come from various sources, whether by others, lived experiences, or cultural and social norms. The dangers of personal bias are reflected in the actions of the individual, as they may include undue stereotyping or hostility toward others. I will explain the implications for such actions in the section on implications of personal bias. But first, I present Erbe's (2019) exploratory case study on personal bias, with a focus on cognitive and perceptual biases.

Introduction: personal bias exploratory case study

In exploring personal bias, we utilize "Intrapersonal Approaches to Conflict: Cognitive and Perceptual Biases,"[57] which can be explored on the level of the individual as it pertains to personal bias. The significance of this case is due to the reflection of cognitive and perceptual bias as part of personal bias. As in the cultural bias case study, I will present reflections on and implications of the case following the case presentation.

Case study: "Intrapersonal Approaches to Conflict: Cognitive and Perceptual Biases"[58]

Background: You receive a call from the ombuds at the local headquarters of a multinational corporation. He asks you to talk with a disgruntled employee (hereinafter called complaining employee). This ombuds normally addresses employee complaints himself, but the last time he attempted to do so, his neutrality was challenged. He reports to the corporate legal department and is consulting with you to ensure neutrality.

Application: Many organizations offer their own conflict resolution services with known and trusted "insiders" acting as ombuds (and mediators.) Imagine yourself in conflict with a university or

---

⁵⁷ Erbe, *Conflict Case Studies.*
⁵⁸ Case adapted as presented in Erbe (2019).

other organization. What are your concerns if asked to work with an "insider"—organizational employee? Propose ideas for addressing these concerns; include parameters or criteria for assessing the appropriateness of "insider" intervention.

Hypothetical case: Privately, you are thrilled that a major corporation, with substantial resources, is requesting your services. You started your business a few years ago and still worry about paying monthly bills. It's refreshing to hear from a client who can afford to pay full market rates for services. You hope this begins a long-term relationship and source of business. The complaining employee gives you a letter detailing his complaints. He is "seriously considering" suing but would rather "work out something mutually beneficial" since he is a new employee and prefers to remain employed on good terms.

Reflections on exploratory case study

The purpose of presenting this case is to demonstrate that individuals have several factors that influence their likelihood of making a decision. As such, by exploring what actions you would take within this situation prior to understanding the bias of the hypothetical individual within the case, you, as the reader, can explore the different considerations that influence our cognitive and perceptual bias in addition to the factors of personal bias that have been described. The additional factors pertaining to personal bias, particularly in terms of cognition and perception, that may impact an individual's decision and judgment within this case include the following:

- Past experiences
- Motivations and goals
- Personal relationships
- Morals and values
- Perceived/anticipated consequences of the action or behavior

In the next section, we explore the implications for personal bias with the use of practical considerations in the health care sector, as presented by Haddad et al. (2019).

Personal Bias Implications

The purpose of presenting these two cases on personal bias is to urge the reader to reflect upon their own personal bias and to explore the role of their personal bias in their decision-making. The presentation of "Intrapersonal Approaches to Conflict: Cognitive and Perceptual Biases"[59] was, therefore, used to demonstrate potential personal biases and how they could directly impact the decisions made in response to a given situation. In presenting the case in health care, beyond understanding that one has personal biases that impact their decision-making, it is essential to consider the impact these personal biases have on other individuals. In the case of health-care practice, Haddad et al. (2019) expressed the recognition of personal biases as essential based on the following:

> Understanding the way personal biases influence us and their effect on our attitudes and conduct are important to the health professional. Whenever bias is present, it affects the type of communication possible between the persons involved and therefore must be recognized as one determining factor in respectful interaction. In some cases, personal bias may produce a positive bias, or "halo effect," on certain individuals; that is, a single characteristic or trait leads to positive global judgments about a person. For example, a patient who is pleasant and cooperative during office visits also could be thought by the health professional to be compliant with therapy

---

[59] Erbe, *Conflict Case Studies.*

because of the halo effect even though the oppo-site could be true…Personal biases can lead to discrimination. Discrimination is negative, different treatment of a person or group. Usually it is derived from prejudice…In this way we see how prejudicial attitudes of health professionals tend to manifest in discriminatory behavior that can have concrete implications for patients regarding the care they receive.[60]

Why is inner bias, as formed by cultural bias, important? On one hand, we have presented, with the support of the cases designed by Erbe (2019), that both cultural and personal biases shape our decisions. On the other hand, we have established that personal and cultural biases also influence our actions toward others and, in some cases, can have a negative effect. I explore further the implications for personal and cultural biases alongside our cognition, judgment, and decision-making in the summary.

Summary

Inner biases in judgment and decision-making

To summarize the importance of bias within interactions between individuals, we return to a reflection on bias from both the patient and health-care professional:

In short, every exchange between a patient and health professional undoubtedly will be influenced by cultural differences and other sources of personal bias. Sometimes these feelings will create an attitude of prejudice and a desire to discriminate. However, despite legal restrictions

---

[60] Haddad, Doherty, and Purtilo, "Chapter 5—Respect in a Diverse Society."

to eliminate discrimination in the health care environment, it occurs craftily and evasively. You must watch for it in yourself and others because both parties involved are inevitably injured by the interaction. Allport warns, "It is a serious error to ascribe prejudice and discrimination to any single taproot, reaching into economic exploitation, social structure, the mores, fear, aggression, sex conflict, or any other favored soil. Prejudice and discrimination may draw nourishment from all these conditions and many others." At the same time, treating people differently because of race, religion, ethnicity, gender, or other attributes does not necessarily imply prejudice and discrimination. Respect for differences includes understanding when those differences should count to benefit patients, how they inform the responses of people, and the process of providing patient-centered, culturally informed care.[61]

The statement presented reflects the complexities of bias in terms of prejudice and discrimination, differential treatment, and the differences in responses to situations, both from the side of the patient and health-care professional. But why do our inner biases, based on cultural and personal bias, have such an impact? I present the answer is twofold. Because cultural and personal bias shapes our inner bias, extending on the point presented at the beginning of this chapter, such biases impact our cognition. A second key point is that our inner biases, although shaping our cognition, are largely unconscious.

Unconscious bias

Differences based on bias have implications for communication, behaviors, and actions between individuals. Nevertheless,

---

[61] Ibid.

unconscious bias, based on the fact that they are not immediately noticeable to the individual, have important implications for our cognition:

> Once you become aware of your often *unconscious biases,* you can more easily avoid being controlled by them in your interactions with others. Unconscious biases influence our interpretation of what we hear and see to conform with previously established beliefs. Furthermore, by becoming aware of your hidden biases, you will be less likely to form inappropriate judgments about…others and more likely to remain sensitive and open to differences that influence your interactions with them.[62]

Although we have described and illustrated the role of bias, including the unconscious nature of bias within decision-making and judgment, the complexity of bias cannot be overlooked. The unavailable role of bias and judgment and decision-making is reflected in the following statement:

> Humans consistently exhibit systematic biases in their judgments. Some of these biases seem to stem from self-enhancing or self-protective motives (e.g., Greenwald, 1980; Myers, 1980). Others may stem from general cognitive shortcuts or heuristics (e.g., Kahneman, Slovic, and Tversky, 1982). Still others seem to reflect an inappropriate sensitivity or insensitivity to certain types of information (e.g., underuse of base-rate information; Kahneman et al., 1982; Nisbett and Ross, 1980). Regardless of their sources, systematic judgmental biases can have serious con-

---

[62] Haddad, "Chapter 5—Respect in a Diverse Society."

sequences (cf. Dawes, 1988; Thaler, 1991), and identifying means of controlling such biases is an important challenge for psychology.[63]

Due to the complexities associated with bias, judgment, and decision-making, scholars have been largely silent in providing an overarching response or theory pertaining to the role of bias and judgment and decision-making. This relative silence is justified given that bias is not only complex but also highly subjective.

Returning to heuristics: bias and cognition

I posit that bias is largely internalized, thereby forming our "inner biases." Beyond reliance on an individual expressing their inner biases, the exploration of inner biases can be conducted by understanding the influence of bias on the actions of an individual, as reflected in their judgment and decision-making. We established in chapter 1 that individuals often make decisions quickly based on such biases, which are influenced by both cultural and personal biases. I conclude by reminding the reader that heuristics are formed by our biases. The inner biases and, in turn, our judgment, decision-making, and behaviors are only produced bias but are influenced by our own cognitive biases. I collectively term these biases and the complex formation of our cognition our "inner biases."

---

[63] Kerr, MacCoun, and Kramer, "Bias in Judgment: Comparing Individuals and Groups," 687.

The Author's Research

Introduction

The exploration of inner biases within this book is a result of the uncovering of this phenomenon within my empirical research on the issue of infertility as a global health issue. Infertility, the inability of a couple to conceive after one year or more of regular unprotected sexual intercourse, is a worldwide health issue.[64] On a macro level,

---

[64] World Health Organization (WHO), *International Classification of Diseases, 11th Revision (ICD-11); Ali et al., "Knowledge, Perceptions and Myths Regarding Infertility Among Selected Adult Population in Pakistan: A Cross-Sectional Study,"* 1–7; Boivin et al., "International Estimates of Infertility Prevalence and Treatment-Seeking: Potential Need and Demand for Infertility Medical Care," 1506–1512; Carter et al., "A Cross-Sectional Cohort Study of Infertile Women Awaiting Oocyte Donation: The Emotional, Sexual, and Quality-of-Life Impact," 711–716; Gurunath et al., "Defining Infertility—A Systematic Review of Prevalence Studies," 575–588; Inhorn, "'The Worms Are Weak' Male Infertility and Patriarchal Paradoxes in Egypt," 236–256; Montazeri, "Infertility and Health Related Quality of Life: Minireview of the Literature,"

some parts of the world struggle with overpopulation.[65] However, on a more micro level, many women struggle with the inability to conceive a child and with issues of infertility.[66] In some countries, infertility has been identified as a solution to overpopulation.[67] However, the focus of the empirical research presented in this book is infertility experienced by women.

Infertility is defined by many researchers as the failure to bear a child after one year of unprotected intercourse.[68] Infertility is a serious public health issue. Infertile couples perceive infertility differently based on their ethnographical background.[69] Beliefs, values,

---

55–58; Ziegler, D., B. Borghese, and C. Chapron, "Endometriosis and Infertility: Pathophysiology and Management," 730–738.

[65] Cousineau and Domar, "Psychological Impact of Infertility," 293–308; Ombelet, "Global Access to Infertility Care in Developing Countries: A Case of Human Rights, Equity and Social Justice," 257–266; Pennings and Mertes, "Ethical Issues in Infertility Treatment," 853–863.

[66] Balen, *Infertility in Practice*; Berger, Paul, and Henshaw, "Women's Experience of Infertility: A Multi-Systemic Perspective," 54–68; Inhorn, "'The Worms Are Weak' Male Infertility and Patriarchal Paradoxes in Egypt," 236–256.

[67] Cousineau and Domar, "Psychological Impact of Infertility," 293–308; Inhorn, "'The Worms Are Weak' Male Infertility and Patriarchal Paradoxes in Egypt," 236–256; Ombelet, "Global Access to Infertility Care in Developing Countries: A Case of Human Rights, Equity and Social Justice," 257–266; Pennings and Mertes, "Ethical Issues in Infertility Treatment," 853–863.

[68] Ali et al., "Knowledge, Perceptions and Myths Regarding Infertility Among Selected Adult Population in Pakistan: A Cross-Sectional Study," 1–7; Boivin et al., "International Estimates of Infertility Prevalence and Treatment-Seeking: Potential Need and Demand for Infertility Medical Care," 1506–1512; Carter et al., "A Cross-Sectional Cohort Study of Infertile Women Awaiting Oocyte Donation: The Emotional, Sexual, and Quality-of-Life Impact," 711–716; Gurunath et al., "Defining Infertility—A Systematic Review of Prevalence Studies," 575–588; Inhorn, "'The Worms Are Weak' Male Infertility and Patriarchal Paradoxes in Egypt," 236–256; Montazeri, "Infertility and Health Related Quality of Life: Minireview of the Literature," 55–58; Ziegler, D., B. Borghese, and C. Chapron, "Endometriosis and Infertility: Pathophysiology and Management," 730–738; Bell, "Constructions of 'Infertility' and Some Lived Experiences of Involuntary Childlessness," 284–295.

[69] Bell, "Constructions of 'Infertility' and Some Lived Experiences of Involuntary Childlessness," 284–295; Greil, McQuillan, and Slauson-Blevins, "The Social Construction of Infertility," 736–746; Greil, Slauson-Blevins, and McQuillan,

traditions, religions, relatives, and many other factors could affect the quality of life of infertile couples. A person's perception of infertility is merged with daily life functioning as a mix of physical, social, emotional, and cognitive activities.[70]

In this chapter, the background to the empirical research to be presented in this book is presented. This background centers on the topic of infertility, with a focus on Arab communities in the United States. From this focus, the topic of inner biases surrounding infertility, the role of culture surrounding these biases, and implications for public health and research more broadly will be presented.

Background to the Topic

As introduced, the topic of our inner biases was developed from the empirical research I conducted on the infertility of Arab American women. To understand the connections between inner biases and the topic of infertility, I present this topic as one which derives from public health but is intertwined with culture. In turn, ideas surrounding infertility are, therefore, closely related to our inner biases, as will be revealed in chapter 4.

In this background to the topic, I present infertility as a public health issue and present the role of culture as playing a key role in the ideas and biases on infertility. Next, I will link these concepts with understanding infertility among women in the Arab culture and within Arab American communities in the United States more spe-

---

"The Experience of Infertility: A Review of Recent Literature," 140–162; Schmid et al., "Infertility Caused by PCOS—Health-Related Quality of Life among Austrian and Moslem Immigrant Women in Austria," 2251–2257.

[70] Bell, "Constructions of 'Infertility' and Some Lived Experiences of Involuntary Childlessness," 284–295; Greil, McQuillan, and Slauson-Blevins, "The Social Construction of Infertility," 736–746; Greil, Slauson-Blevins, and McQuillan, "The Experience of Infertility: A Review of Recent Literature," 140–162; Schmid et al., "Infertility Caused by PCOS—Health-Related Quality of Life among Austrian and Moslem Immigrant Women in Austria," 2251–2257.

cifically. This background will provide a foundation for understanding the perception of Arab American women towards their infertility.

Infertility as a public health issue

Infertility is a public health issue that impacts countries and communities on a global scale. Infertility affects approximately 60–168 million individuals worldwide.[71] More recent estimates place this number at 48 million couples and 186 million individuals with infertility globally.[72] This number suggests that an estimated one in ten couples suffer from primary or secondary infertility. The World Health Organization (WHO) has estimated that approximately 10 percent of women experience infertility and subfertility, which presents this as a global public health concern.[73] Nearly 30 percent of infertility issues occur in developing countries.[74] Added to this problem is that the overall burden of subfertility and infertility rates is likely to be underestimated.[75]

According to the Centers for Disease Control and Prevention (CDC, 2019), based on 2015–2017 estimates, in the United States, 8.8 percent of married women aged fifteen to forty-nine are infertile.[76] Among women of all marital statuses, 13.1 percent have

---

[71] Rutstein and Shah, "Infecundity, Infertility, and Childlessness in Developing Countries (No. 9)"; Ali et al., "Knowledge, Perceptions and Myths Regarding Infertility Among Selected Adult Population in Pakistan: A Cross-Sectional Study," 1–7; Cousineau and Domar, "Psychological Impact of Infertility," 293–308.

[72] Mascarenhas et al., "National, Regional, and Global Trends in Infertility Prevalence Since 1990: A Systematic Analysis of 277 Health Surveys"; Rutstein and Shah, "Infecundity, Infertility, and Childlessness in Developing Countries (No. 9)"; Boivin et al., "International Estimates of Infertility Prevalence and Treatment-Seeking: Potential Need and Demand for Infertility Medical Care," 1506–1512.

[73] World Health Organization (WHO), "Infertility Is a Global Public Health Issues."

[74] Cousineau and Domar, "Psychological Impact of Infertility," 293–308.

[75] World Health Organization (WHO), "Infertility Is a Global Public Health Issues."

[76] Centers for Disease Control (CDC), "Infertility."

impaired fecundity, which is the difficulty or impossibility of getting pregnant or carrying a pregnancy to term.[77] Among married women, this percentage increases to 16.2 percent of women with impaired fecundity, based on 2015–2017 estimates.[78] These numbers are an increase from the CDC's 2013 estimates in which approximately 1.5 million married women are diagnosed with infertility, accounting for 6.0 percent of the total number of married women. Being infertile is one of the most stressful conditions a woman can experience.[79] For this reason, evaluating the status of infertility as a common health issue is very complicated, and many factors influence a woman's decision to receive treatment.

The role of culture in understanding infertility: a need for further research

The burden of infertility as a public health issue targets both females and males equally.[80] However, in different societies, cultures, and communities, people blame the woman at first as the main cause of infertility problems.[81] Public health can benefit from studying

---

[77] Ibid.

[78] Ibid.

[79] Benyamini, Gozlan, and Weissman, "Normalization as a Strategy for Maintaining Quality of Life while Coping with Infertility in a Pronatalist Culture," 871-879; Martins et al., "Direct and Indirect Effects of Perceived Social Support on Women's Infertility-Related Stress," 2113–2121; Peterson et al., "Coping Processes of Couples Experiencing Infertility," 227–239; Sormunen et al., "Infertility-Related Communication and Coping Strategies among Women Affected by Primary or Secondary Infertility," e335–e344; Amini, Ghorbani, and Afshar, "The Comparison of Infertility Stress and Perceived Social Support in Infertile Women and Spouses of Infertile Men," 74–85.

[80] Inhorn and Van Balen, eds. *Infertility Around the Globe: New Thinking on Childlessness, Gender, and Reproductive Technologies.*

[81] Deribe et al., "Infertility Perceived Causes and Experiences in Rural South West Ethiopia"; Inhorn, *Infertility and Patriarchy: The Cultural Politics of Gender and Family Life in Egypt;* Kimani and Olenja, "Infertility: Cultural Dimensions and Impact on Women in Selected Communities in Kenya," 200–214; Peterson et al., "Coping Processes of Couples Experiencing Infertility," 227–239.

each population separately, taking into account different cultural backgrounds to understand how women perceive their infertility.

In a recent qualitative study, Höbek Akarsu and Kızılkaya Beji (2019) noted that women's health is associated with their ability to reproduce.[82] Women also tend to link their infertility to stress and religion,[83] particularly in Arab cultures.[84] Based on this link between the social pressures on women to reproduce, there is a stigma surrounding the infertility of women.[85] These stigmas lead to negative self-perception, feeling of inadequacy (internalized stigma), social isolation, postponing medical treatment, impacted marital relationships, and reduced quality of life for women with infertility.[86]

Consistent with Höbek Akarsu and Kızılkaya Beji (2019), in quantitative, descriptive-analytic study in Turkey, Yüksekol et al. (2020) found that there was a negative, moderate, significant correlation between gender perception and infertility distress among Turkish women.[87] Specifically, infertility distress resulted in negative psychological and emotional impacts. As a result, Yüksekol et al. (2020) concluded that gender perceptions must be addressed in addressing infertility for women given the impact of such perceptions on infertility distress outcomes.[88] Negative outcomes associated with infertility include reduced self-esteem, sexual distress or stress,

---

[82] Höbek and Kızılkaya, "Spiritual and Religious Issues of Stigmatization Women with Infertility: A Qualitative Study," 256–267.

[83] Ibid.

[84] Ibrahim et al., "Perceptions of Infertility among Women in United Arab Emirates: A Qualitative Study."

[85] Satheesan and Satyanarayana, "Quality of Marital Relationship, Partner Violence, Psychological Distress, and Resilience in Women with Primary Infertility," 734–739.

[86] Höbek and Kızılkaya, "Spiritual and Religious Issues of Stigmatization Women with Infertility: A Qualitative Study," 256–267; Gonzalez, "Infertility as a Transformational Process: A Framework for Psychotherapeutic Support of Infertile Women," 619–633; Ibrahim et al., "Perceptions of Infertility among Women in United Arab Emirates: A Qualitative Study."

[87] Yüksekol, Duman, and Ozan, "The Relationship between Gender Perception Levels and Infertility Distress of Infertile Women."

[88] Ibid.

depression, guilt, anxiety, frustration, emotional distress, and relationship problems.[89]

Many studies have been conducted to study infertility.[90] Most of these studies were large quantitative surveys that address the issue of infertility to evaluate the incidence and occurrence of both types of infertility, assess the causes of infertility, and evaluate treatments.[91] In African culture, women perceive infertility as an evil, supernatural power affecting their health.[92] As with the African countries, Middle Eastern countries (representing a section of the Arab world) have been also reported to have their own ways to perceive infertility, as well as different strategies for seeking treatments. African countries and Middle Eastern countries perceive infertility differently.

When addressing the Arab countries, it is critical to keep in mind that this region includes twenty-two countries: the Gulf area countries, Middle East countries, and other countries that speak Arabic, such as Libya, Yemen, Tunisia, Egypt, and others. Though not all populations perceive infertility the same way, common mental

---

[89] Vitale et al., "Psychology of Infertility and Assisted Reproductive Treatment: The Italian Situation," 1–3; Zayed and El-Hadidy, "Sexual Satisfaction and Self-Esteem in Women with Primary Infertility," 1–5; Zayed and El-Hadidy, "Sexual Satisfaction and Self-Esteem in Women with Primary Infertility," 1–5.

[90] Deribe et al., "Infertility Perceived Causes and Experiences in Rural South West Ethiopia"; Hollos et al., "The Problem of Infertility in High Fertility Populations: Meanings, Consequences and Coping Mechanisms in Two Nigerian Communities, 2061–2068; Schmid et al., "Infertility Caused by PCOS—Health-Related Quality of Life among Austrian and Moslem Immigrant Women in Austria," 2251–2257; Sudha and Reddy, "Causes of Female Infertility: A Cross-Sectional Study," 119–123.

[91] Volgsten et al., "Risk Factors for Psychiatric Disorders in Infertile Women and Men Undergoing In Vitro Fertilization Treatment," 1088–1096.

[92] Deribe et al., "Infertility Perceived Causes and Experiences in Rural South West Ethiopia;" de Kok, "Infertility in Malawi: Exploring Its Impact and Social Consequences"; Dyer et al., "'Men Leave Me as I Cannot Have Children': Women's Experiences with Involuntary Childlessness, 1663–1668; Dyer et al., "'You Are a Man because You Have Children': Experiences, Reproductive Health Knowledge and Treatment-Seeking Behaviour among Men Suffering from Couple Infertility in South Africa," 960–967; Dyer, Lombard, and Van der Spuy, "Psychological Distress among Men Suffering from Couple Infertility in South Africa: A Quantitative Assessment," 2821–2826.

and emotional problems are found in infertile individuals, such as depression, stress, feelings of insecurity, and many more. Most studies conducted to evaluate and assess infertility in Arabic countries focused mainly on understanding causes, symptoms, and treatments. Some other studies focused on the psychological influence of infertility on individuals.[93] Only a few studies explored the psychological effects of infertility on individuals.

According to many studies, infertility can result in stress, depression, and insecurity in infertile women, as well as social issues and marital problems.[94] Although many studies have evaluated the causes of and treatments for infertility, few studies evaluate individual perceptions of infertility. Moreover, whereas a few existing studies highlight perceptions of infertility in developed countries, such perceptions in developing countries still need to be evaluated.[95] Overall, because of this gap in the literature, there is limited knowledge about the perceptions of individuals of infertility.

Arab communities in the United States

The role of culture also affects the ability of a woman to cope with the diagnosis of infertility.[96] This is particularly true of Arab

---

[93] Moghaddam et al., "New Ultrahigh Affinity Host—Guest Complexes of Cucurbit [7] Uril with Bicyclo [2.2. 2] Octane and Adamantane Guests: Thermodynamic Analysis and Evaluation of m2 Affinity Calculations," 3570–3581.

[94] Peterson et al., "Coping Processes of Couples Experiencing Infertility," 227–239; Hollos et al., "The Problem of Infertility in High Fertility Populations: Meanings, Consequences and Coping Mechanisms in Two Nigerian Communities, 2061–2068; Martins et al., "Direct and Indirect Effects of Perceived Social Support on Women's Infertility-Related Stress," 2113–2121.

[95] Volgsten et al., "Risk Factors for Psychiatric Disorders in Infertile Women and Men Undergoing In Vitro Fertilization Treatment," 1088–1096; Macer and Taylor, "Endometriosis and Infertility: A Review of the Pathogenesis and Treatment of Endometriosis-Associated Infertility," 535–549.

[96] Greil, McQuillan, and Slauson-Blevins, "The Social Construction of Infertility," 736–746; Bell, "Constructions of 'Infertility' and Some Lived Experiences of Involuntary Childlessness," 284–295; Greil, Slauson-Blevins, and McQuillan, "The Experience of Infertility: A Review of Recent Literature, 140–162;

American women, who are highly influenced by their cultures, norms, and traditions. According to the US census (2003), 1.2 million Arabs reside in the United States. This population accounts for approximately 0.42 percent of the total population of the US. This percentage indicates that Arab women may not be recognized as having different health care needs than other ethnic or religious groups that make up the majority of the US population. Most of the decisions these women make are based on what their culture frame as right and wrong.[97] For this reason, it is important to understand how these women think and behave to understand their attitudes in their decision-making. Understanding the lived experiences and perspectives of Arab American women who experience infertility is important and addresses a gap in the literature relating to culture, beliefs, and infertility for this ethnic minority in the United States.

While many states (Michigan, California, New York, Florida, New Jersey, Illinois, Texas, and Ohio) have Arab populations, this research will focus on the issue of infertility in women who live in Michigan, specifically in Dearborn, the city with the largest Arab population as of the 2010 United States census, at the time of conducting the empirical research upon which this book is based. Arab communities are among the fastest-growing communities in the United States. They are also one of the most complex communities among foreign groups in the US because they are so divergent in traditions, languages, religions, and beliefs. In the past few years, studies have focused on African, Asian, and Hispanic communities, but few have looked at Arab communities in the United States. This could be due to the cultural complexity of Arabic communities. For this reason, studies addressing Arab populations focus only on one specific health issue, such as mental health, children's health, and sexual health.

One of the concepts that may vary among different cultures and communities is the concept of a "family." In Arab communities, the

---

Schmid et al., "Infertility Caused by PCOS—Health-Related Quality of Life among Austrian and Moslem Immigrant Women in Austria," 2251–2257.

[97] Greil, McQuillan, and Slauson-Blevins, "The Social Construction of Infertility," 736–746.

concept of family is highly respected and is considered to be a vital part of life.[98] Pregnant women are always surrounded by attention and care and garner respect from both their family and society. On the other hand, infertility is considered a dishonor for any married couple. Infertility can cause stress and pressure on a married couple and can lead to divorce in many Arabic societies.[99] Arabs emphasize the importance of a family in an individual's life and his/her relations with the surroundings (other family members, the public, and his/her friends).

Religious beliefs play a vital role in determining individual behaviors. The majority of the Arab women who live in Dearborn, Michigan, are Muslims, as reported by the Arab American Institute (2014). Consequently, it is important to have an overview of what Islam says about health. According to the Koran (the Islam's holy book), an individual's health is a priority, and it is the individual's duty to take care of his/her health through personal hygiene, good nutrition, and exercise. Nonetheless, many Arabic women find it difficult to take care of their health and to seek health care from male health providers.

Arab women are sensitive when it comes to exposing their bodies to a male physician or even discussing a sensitive health issue in front of male professionals.[100] Infertility is one of the most embarrassing health problems an Arabic woman can face. This could be related to the fact that infertility causes feelings of "shame" or "incompleteness" or because she might be blamed for their infertility. For this reason, this study will draw attention to Arab women as the target population to understand their perspectives toward infertility.

---

[98] Henry et al., "Perceived Parental Acculturation Behaviors and Control as Predictors of Subjective Well-Being in Arab American College Students," 28–34.

[99] Moghaddam et al., "New Ultrahigh Affinity Host—Guest Complexes of Cucurbit [7] Uril with Bicyclo [2.2. 2] Octane and Adamantane Guests: Thermodynamic Analysis and Evaluation of m2 Affinity Calculations," 3570–3581.

[100] Crabtree, "Culture, Gender and the Influence of Social Change amongst Emirati Families in the United Arab Emirates," 575–588.

Introduction to the Empirical Research

Arab women, although a minority in the US, are greatly influenced by cultural and social factors. In the Arab community, getting married is one of the most respected steps toward building a family and having children. As a result, being infertile leads to shame.[101] There is a paucity of literature about how infertility is perceived among Arab women living in the United States. Accordingly, I designed the empirical study to understand how Arab women in Dearborn, Michigan, perceive being infertile.

Religious beliefs play a vital role in determining individual behaviors. The majority of the Arab women who live in Dearborn, Michigan, are Muslims, as reported by the Arab American Institute (2014). Consequently, it is important to have an overview of what Islam says about health. According to the Koran (the Islam's holy book), an individual's health is a priority, and it is the individual's duty to take care of his/her health through personal hygiene, good nutrition, and exercise. Nonetheless, many Arabic women find it difficult to take care of their health and to seek health care from male health providers.

Arab women are sensitive when it comes to exposing their bodies to a male physician or even discussing a sensitive health issue in front of male professionals.[102] Infertility is one of the most embarrassing health problems an Arabic woman can face. This could be related to the fact that infertility causes feelings of "shame" or "incompleteness" or because she might be blamed for their infertility. For this reason, this study will draw attention to Arab women as the target population to understand their perspectives toward infertility.

---

[101] Dierickx, "'With the Kanyaleng and the Help of God, You Don't Feel Ashamed': Women Experiencing Infertility in Casamance, Senegal," 1–16; Crabtree, "Culture, Gender and the Influence of Social Change amongst Emirati Families in the United Arab Emirates," 575–588.

[102] Ibid.

Purpose of the empirical research

The purpose of the empirical study was to be able to understand how Arab women who live in Dearborn, Michigan, feel about infertility and to understand their concerns and worries about their health status. Consequently, health-care providers can have a more comprehensive understanding of the specific needs this minority population has. In exploring this phenomenon, this study sought to understand the issues and feelings of Arab women living in Dearborn, Michigan, toward infertility. The overarching research questions for this study were:

> RQ1: What are the perspectives of Arab women
> toward infertility?
> RQ2: How do Arab women see the impacts of
> their infertility on their future?

Methodology

This study followed a qualitative method to evaluate and understand how Arab women perceive their infertility status. Face-to-face interviews were used to collect their responses. The qualitative approach was used to illuminate the quality-of-life variables or measures that were linked to infertility. This study followed the ethnographic approach.

The ethnographic approach focuses on explaining and describing a group of individuals who share the same cultural background, beliefs, and, in this case, the same health issue experiences. Ethnographic studies have been used widely in qualitative research to assess the importance of different cultures and how different populations from culturally diverse populations behave differently. The use of ethnographic methodology also allowed me to yield deep insights regarding this phenomenon, which led to the growing understanding and exploration of the inner biases surrounding the perceptions of infertility among Arab women.

Significance of the empirical study

The impact of infertility and its treatment on women is of great concern to public health officials.[103] Women are affected more than men, and infertility treatment is one of the most difficult experiences in a woman's life.[104] As a result, public health staff and health-care providers should be very familiar with the psychosocial factors surrounding their patients.[105] It is recommended that health-care providers, when dealing with patients, have the skills and ability to understand their patients' different backgrounds.[106] Unfortunately, many health-care professionals do not show familiarity with the patient's background. This empirical study evaluated Arab women's perceptions of infertility and, thus, could provide health-care professionals with important information about a neglected population. Another insight yielded from this research was the importance of inner biases surrounding fertility—the focus of this book.

Summary

As reflected in this chapter, the issue of infertility is a public health concern on a global level. Moreover, there are many cultural factors, particularly for women, that play a role in the way in which women view infertility. In chapters 1 and 2, I established the link between personal and cultural biases in shaping our inner biases. Additionally, through cases and an overview of the inner cognitive workings of bias, we explored the impact that bias has on shaping our

---

[103] Peterson et al., "Coping Processes of Couples Experiencing Infertility," 227–239; Berghuis and Stanton, "Adjustment to a Dyadic Stressor: A Longitudinal Study of Coping and Depressive Symptoms in Infertile Couples over an Insemination Attempt," 433–438; Burns, Covington, and Kempers, *Infertility Counseling.*

[104] Crabtree, "Culture, Gender and the Influence of Social Change amongst Emirati Families in the United Arab Emirates," 575–588.

[105] Ali et al., "Effect of Acacia Gum on Blood Pressure in Rats with Adenine-Induced Chronic Renal Failure," 1176–1180.

[106] Ibid.

thoughts and ideas—thereby forming our inner biases. In chapter 4, building upon this link, I will present the findings of my research to demonstrate how inner biases manifest using a real-world empirical case. From this case, we will further link this case to the arguments presented for inner biases to demonstrate how they are woven together in the fabrics of society and within ourselves and manifest within phenomena such as health outcomes and public health priority areas.

CHAPTER 4

Overcoming Inner Biases

Introduction

Recognizing that inner biases exist, the question of how to address such biases emerges. Using the empirical case of infertility in chapter 3, it is evident not only that inner biases exist but also that they may result in negative impacts for those toward which such biases are directed. The empirical example demonstrates that inner biases can be observed and identified by an external entity.

In this chapter, I explore how such inner biases can be overcome and the extent to which such inner biases can be transformed by individuals and communities, in the case of collective inner biases. To explore the concept of overcoming inner bias, I reflect again upon the theory and concepts presented in chapter 1 to serve as the foundation for deconstructing the concept of overcoming inner biases. Specifically, I will return to the sources of inner biases and the connections between inner biases and decision-making, intuitive judgment, and critical thinking. In exploring such connections, using the case of women's infertility in Arab communities in the United States, we will return to (a) how views toward women's infertility are shaped by inner biases and (b) how such inner biases can be overcome.

Overcoming Inner Biases at the Source

As established in chapter 1 and demonstrated in the case of infertility in women presented in chapter 3, inner bias includes an individual's perceived background, and perceived societal and cultural stereotypes will be described regarding their impact on decision-making, both consciously and subconsciously. As such, inner bias consists of both cultural and personal sources that influence such bias. Both will be explored in the subsections below.

Overcoming Personal Bias

Personal bias is based on our interpretations and judgment. Beyond our own interpretations and judgments as individuals, these biases are often intertwined with cultural bias and cultural relativity, making them difficult to separate from the biases of the individual.[107] As social beings, our personal biases are often shaped by social norms, which create expectations of our behavior and, therefore, shape personal values and beliefs.[108] For this reason, I turn to cultural bias as a foundation for targeting and overcoming inner biases.

---

[107] Mccullagh, "Bias in Historical Description, Interpretation, and Explanation," 39–66.

[108] Cislaghi et al., "Changing Social Norms: The Importance of 'Organized Diffusion' for Scaling Up Community Health Promotion and Women Empowerment Interventions," 936–946; Bell and Cox, "Social Norms: Do We Love Norms Too Much?" 28–46; Mackie et al., *What Are Social Norms? How Are They Measured?*; Miller and Prentice, "Changing Norms to Change Behavior," 339–361; Saxena, "The 'Reference Group' Concept," 155–164.

Overcoming Cultural Bias

In connecting the concepts presented in chapter 1 with the empirical case in chapter 3, the issue of cultural bias is reflected in the behaviors, expectations, and beliefs of communities, which consist of individuals. Couples perceive infertility differently based on their ethnographical background.[109] Beliefs, values, traditions, religions, relatives, and many other factors could affect the quality of life of infertile couples. A person's perception of infertility is merged with daily life functioning as a mix of physical, social, emotional, and cognitive activities.[110]

Overcoming Inner Biases
Returning to Decision-Making, Intuitive Judgement, and Critical Thinking

Due to cognitive bias, inner biases impact decision-making, intuitive judgment, and critical thinking of individuals, which is directly related to the behavior of individuals both at an individual and community level. The reason for this is based on the connection between the thinking mind and the physical mind, which is responsible for the neurophysiological activities that correspond with the memory, thinking, and information processing that occurs within

---

[109] Bell, "Constructions of 'Infertility' and Some Lived Experiences of Involuntary Childlessness," 284–295; Greil, McQuillan, and Slauson-Blevins, "The Social Construction of Infertility," 736–746; Greil, Slauson-Blevins, and McQuillan, "The Experience of Infertility: A Review of Recent Literature," 140–162; Schmid et al., "Infertility Caused by PCOS—Health-Related Quality of Life among Austrian and Moslem Immigrant Women in Austria," 2251–2257.

[110] Bell, "Constructions of 'Infertility' and Some Lived Experiences of Involuntary Childlessness," 284–295; Greil, McQuillan, and Slauson-Blevins, "The Social Construction of Infertility," 736–746; Greil, Slauson-Blevins, and McQuillan, "The Experience of Infertility: A Review of Recent Literature," 140–162; Schmid et al., "Infertility Caused by PCOS—Health-Related Quality of Life among Austrian and Moslem Immigrant Women in Austria," 2251–2257.

the thinking mind.[111] To overcome inner biases, both personal and cultural sources of bias must be addressed. To understand how such inner biases are present within an individual, their decision-making, intuitive judgment, and critical thinking based on such inner biases need to be understood and targeted alongside the sources of inner biases.

Decision-making

As explained in chapter 1, decision-making is influenced by judgment, which is impacted by bias. In reflecting on decision-making as a means of overcoming inner biases, it perhaps is one of the most transparent to tackle. As decision-making may result in external behaviors, such behaviors can be observed, both by the individual and external observers, as a means of recognizing, reflecting upon, and changing the decision-making that results in such behaviors.

To address decision-making that has been impacted by inner biases, the decision-making process of an individual can be examined to understand how they make decisions and, importantly, their justification for such decisions. Having an individual make a decision and explain such a decision allows them to reflect upon the reasoning and cognitive processes involved in making their choice. In doing so, the underlying biases associated with making the decision can be identified and addressed to overcome them.

Understanding decision-making can also be conducted on a collective level by exploring the decision-making of a group of individuals, identifying their justifications for such decisions, and reflecting upon such justifications or explanations. Based on this reflection process, individuals can then be informed of and educated about their biases and the impact of such biases. Individuals must then be informed of how they can change such biases in future decisions.

To demonstrate how decision-making can be tackled, we return to the empirical example provided. In the case of infertility in women, if a woman is blamed or is treated negatively concerning her

---

[111] Solso, MacLin, and MacLin, *Cognitive Psychology*.

infertility, either by herself or others, a decision may be made based on the perceived negative connotations of infertility, which may then be directed toward a woman experiencing infertility. The reason for this connection is due to the influence of cultural bias, which shapes social expectations of behaviors and, therefore, impacts the decisions individuals may make based on such expectations. As discussed previously, the decisions Arab women make are based on what their culture frame as right and wrong.[112] Therefore, there is a link between how these women think based on their culture and beliefs, which, in turn, shape their attitudes, decisions, and potentially their behaviors.

As infertility is a global public health issue,[113] the behaviors that may be negatively impacted based on this phenomenon include those related to health-seeking behaviors and may also pertain to gender-based violence and stigmatization. In other words, if infertility in women is viewed negatively due to inner biases, women may decide not to seek out health-care services pertaining to their fertility. Health seeking may be limited both among those who may suspect that they may experience infertility and, in general, among women in need of reproductive health services due to such inner bias. Health seeking is, therefore, an area in which decision-making associated with infertility can be targeted among this group, and education can

---

[112] Greil, McQuillan, and Slauson-Blevins, "The Social Construction of Infertility," 736–746.

[113] World Health Organization (WHO), *International Classification of Diseases, 11th Revision (ICD-11);* Ali et al., "Knowledge, Perceptions and Myths regarding Infertility among Selected Adult Population in Pakistan: A Cross-Sectional Study," 1–7; Boivin et al., "International Estimates of Infertility Prevalence and Treatment-Seeking: Potential Need and Demand for Infertility Medical Care," 1506–1512; Carter et al., "A Cross-Sectional Cohort Study of Infertile Women Awaiting Oocyte Donation: The Emotional, Sexual, and Quality-of-Life Impact," 711–716; Gurunath et al., "Defining Infertility—A Systematic Review of Prevalence Studies," 575–588; Inhorn, "'The Worms Are Weak' Male Infertility and Patriarchal Paradoxes in Egypt," 236–256; Montazeri, "Infertility and Health-Related Quality of Life: Minireview of the Literature," 55–58; Ziegler, Borghese, and Chapron, "Endometriosis and Infertility: Pathophysiology and Management," 730–738.

be provided to help individuals overcome the inner biases pertaining to their decision-making.

Health-seeking behavior is linked to inner biases because health-seeking, that is, deciding to go to a health-care provider and to receive health information, involves a decision-making process. If an individual views infertility negatively or believes infertility is shaped by the cultural framing of "right and wrong,"[114] within their decision-making process, they may reject the decision to seek care associated with infertility and potentially broadly associated with reproductive health. Such a view that the decision to seek health-care services is not based in fact but rather based on the perception, linked to inner biases, that such a decision would be perceived negatively. In this case, this decision is likely to negatively impact women and is intertwined with intuitive judgment. As decision-making is founded in cognitive thinking, negative views toward infertility in women may not only be linked to one's own decision-making but can extend to judgments and thoughts toward others.

Intuitive judgment

In comparison to decision-making, intuitive judgment presents a greater challenge as it involves the more "inner" aspects of inner bias. Although intuitive judgment is related to decision-making and may ultimately result in external behaviors reflective of inner bias, in many cases, intuitive judgments may remain decisions that are not outwardly expressed in the form of behaviors. The reason is due to intuitive judgment being a subjective internal feeling or "gut feeling."

Given that intuitive judgment does not necessarily result in an outward behavior or decision, it may not be recognized by the individual. To overcome inner biases associated with intuitive judgment, observation of the individual's behaviors associated with a particular target of interest (such as infertility, health-seeking, etc.) can be utilized in addition to making observations of the behaviors of

---

[114] Greil, McQuillan, and Slauson-Blevins, "The Social Construction of Infertility," 736–746.

those within their community. For instance, if an individual or group views or behaves an individual, topic, object, or other phenomenon associated with the target negatively, such a view can be explored to determine whether it is a judgment or "gut feeling" that underlies such behaviors or views. The exploration of intuitive judgment based on inner biases is, therefore, based on outward expressions (behaviors) including voiced opinions, body language, etc. that may reflect such inner biases.

In our case example, an individual may make a judgment about women experiencing infertility or about infertility in general but may not outwardly express their intuitive judgment. Further to this point, this intuitive feeling toward women's infertility may result in a subjective internal feeling that is negative. However, such a negative subjective intuitive judgment toward women experiencing infertility is likely not based on objective facts about women's infertility. As the World Health Organization (WHO) has estimated that approximately 10 percent of women experience infertility and subfertility,[115] it is likely that approximately one in ten women within the Arab community in the United States may experience infertility or subfertility. However, due to intuitive judgments toward infertility, likely, the issue is not discussed due to the potential fear of judgment. In this case, to understand intuitive judgment, individuals within this community could be asked about their views toward infertile women. Moreover, their actions or statements regarding known infertile women could be used to identify intuitive judgment. As with decision-making, inner biases within intuitive judgment, once identified, must then be revealed to the individuals or group, and education about the means of overcoming such biases must be discussed.

Critical thinking

As in the other aspects of cognition discussed, critical thinking is often biased by one's prior thinking and beliefs. Critical think-

---

[115] World Health Organization (WHO), "Infertility Is a Global Public Health Issues."

ing involves the analysis of factual information, which should be an objective process.[116] However, the process of critical thinking is often biased despite the evidence presented.[117] The challenge is that critical thinking allows individuals to evaluate evidence independent of one's own biases. Returning to the quote presented in chapter 1, "virtually all measures of critical thinking try to assess the ability to avoid reasoning that is too biased by prior opinion and prior belief (e.g., Ennis, Millman, and Tomko, 1985; Facione, 1992; Norris and Ennis, 1989; Watson and Glaser, 1980),"[118] to overcome inner biases in critical thinking, biases' reasoning must be overcome to retain objective thinking based on evidence and fact. However, there is evidence that presenting factual information and even providing economic incentives to change behavior alone is not effective.[119]

In our example, revealing the fact that approximately 10 percent of women experience infertility and subfertility[120] and providing an incentive to change harmful practices alone is likely to not be effective in changing practices. The reason is based on the urge to

---

[116] West, Stanovich, and Toplak, "Heuristics and Biases as Measures of Critical Thinking: Associations with Cognitive Ability and Thinking Dispositions," 930–941; Ennis, *Critical Thinking;* Ennis, Millman, and Tomko, *Cornell Critical Thinking Tests;* Facione, *California Critical Thinking Skills Test & California Critical Thinking Dispositions Inventory;* Facione, *Critical Thinking: What It Is and Why It Counts;* Norris, and Ennis, *Evaluating Critical Thinking.*

[117] West, Stanovich, and Toplak, "Heuristics and Biases as Measures of Critical Thinking: Associations with Cognitive Ability and Thinking Dispositions," 930–941; Ennis, *Critical Thinking;* Ennis, Millman, and Tomko, *Cornell Critical Thinking Tests;* Facione, *California Critical Thinking Skills Test & California Critical Thinking Dispositions Inventory;* Facione, *Critical Thinking: What It Is and Why It Counts;* Norris, and Ennis, *Evaluating Critical Thinking.*

[118] West, Stanovich, and Toplak, "Heuristics and Biases as Measures of Critical Thinking: Associations with Cognitive Ability and Thinking Dispositions," 930–941.

[119] Gelfand, and Jackson, "From One Mind to Many: The Emerging Science of Cultural Norms," 175–181; Kumar et al., "Enculturating Science: Community-Centric Design of Behavior Change Interactions for Accelerating Health Impact," 393–415.

[120] World Health Organization (WHO), "Infertility Is a Global Public Health Issues."

resist reasoning based on the bias from prior opinion and belief.[121] Similarly, telling individuals that negative practices or thoughts pertaining to women's infertility (i.e., avoiding health-seeking) is a start to mitigating the biases but may not be effective along in changing such inner biases.

At the level of critical thinking, in addition to targeting the individual and overcoming their personal biases, the reference group or source of inner biases must also be targeted. Individuals often behave based on anticipated social rewards, desire to express membership within their group, or force by individuals that have power over them.[122] Therefore, the reference group is critical to changing the network of individuals that share the norm.[123] Without targeting the reference group, individuals will likely resist changing inner biases despite critical thinking due to expectations based on social norms. With this issue in mind, a public health solution to overcoming inner biases is presented next.

---

[121] West, Stanovich, and Toplak, "Heuristics and Biases as Measures of Critical Thinking: Associations with Cognitive Ability and Thinking Dispositions," 930–941.

[122] Cislaghi et al., "Changing Social Norms: The Importance of 'Organized Diffusion' for Scaling Up Community Health Promotion and Wwomen Empowerment Interventions," 936–946; Bell and Cox, "Social Norms: Do We Love Norms Too Much?" 28–46; Mackie et al., *What Are Social Norms? How Are They Measured?*; Miller, and Prentice, "Changing Norms to Change Behavior," 339–361; Saxena, "The 'Reference Group' Concept," 155–164.

[123] Cislaghi et al., "Changing Social Norms: The Importance of 'Organized Diffusion' for Scaling Up Community Health Promotion and Women Empowerment Interventions," 936–946; Bell and Cox, "Social Norms: Do We Love Norms Too Much?" 28–46; Mackie et al., *What Are Social Norms? How Are They Measured?*; Miller, and Prentice, "Changing Norms to Change Behavior," 339–361; Saxena, "The 'Reference Group' Concept," 155–164.

Overcoming Inner Biases
A Public Health Solution

Addressing cultural courses of inner bias involves changing biases that are collectively held among a group of individuals. To change such beliefs, the group must be made aware of such biases, the potential sources of such biases (traditions, culture, religion, etc.), and the impact of such biases (i.e., negative outcomes that affect the group). As groups are collectively responsible for shaping their beliefs and biases, targeting bias in individuals is necessary but not sufficient. The reason is that if a change in bias rooted in culture is not accepted by the group, there is a risk that it will be rejected, thereby resulting in the group returning to or continuing to maintain the bias.

In public health, an approach that is commonly used is behavior change communication.[124] Behavior change communication is effective particularly in addressing gender-based violence and intimate partner violence, challenges pertaining to negative gender norms and views. Behavior change communication involves educating and engaging individuals to target and change harmful behaviors and beliefs.[125]

---

[124] Roy et al., "Transfers, Behavior Change Communication, and Intimate Partner Violence: Postprogram Evidence from Rural Bangladesh," 865–877; Suzor et al., "Human Rights by Design: The Responsibilities of Social Media Platforms to Address Gender-Based Violence Online," 84–103; Crooks et al., "Preventing Gender-Based Violence among Adolescents and Young Adults: Lessons from 25 Years of Program Development and Evaluation," 29–55; Casey et al., "Gender Transformative Approaches to Engaging Men in Gender-Based Violence Prevention: A Review and Conceptual Model," 231–246.

[125] Roy et al., "Transfers, Behavior Change Communication, and Intimate Partner Violence: Postprogram Evidence from Rural Bangladesh," 865–877; Suzor et al., "Human Rights by Design: The Responsibilities of Social Media Platforms to Address Gender-Based Violence Online," 84–103; Crooks et al., "Preventing Gender-Based Violence among Adolescents and Young Adults: Lessons from 25 Years of Program Development and Evaluation," 29–55; Cislaghi et al., "Changing Social Norms: The Importance of 'Organized Diffusion' for Scaling Up Community Health Promotion and Women Empowerment Interventions," 936–946.

Changing Social Norms to Tackle Inner Biases

The link between cultural and personal sources of inner biases reflects the overlap between one's personal biases and the influences of social norms.[126] Social norms are the unwritten rules of what is considered acceptable behavior among group members.[127] These unwritten rules chape the choices and actions of individuals within the group due to their belief in such norms.[128] Researchers have noted that harmful practices (behaviors) are often sustained by social norms, which are based on collective beliefs.[129] Similar to behavior change communication, one means of addressing harmful practices is to target social norms as the underlying cause of such practices. Community discussions have been implemented as an effective means of changing social norms.

Community discussions involve engaging members of the same group to identify local practices and the norms that sustain such practices.[130] Within this approach, the practices are renegotiated to achieve the improved health, well-being, and empowerment of the group.[131] The renegotiation, therefore, involves the transformation of existing social norms, such as gender. Gender transformative approaches have also been found to be beneficial in changing gender norms and views by engaging men.[132] Women empowerment interventions, which are focused on promoting the autonomy and rights of women, have also been found to be beneficial in changing

---

[126] Cislaghi et al., "Changing Social Norms: The Importance of 'Organized Diffusion' for Scaling Up Community Health Promotion and Women Empowerment Interventions," 936–946.

[127] Ibid.

[128] Ibid.

[129] Ibid.

[130] Casey et al., "Gender Transformative Approaches to Engaging Men in Gender-Based Violence Prevention: A Review and Conceptual Model," 231–246; Linos et al., "Influence of Community Social Norms on Spousal Violence: A Population-Based Multilevel Study of Nigerian Women," 148–155.

[131] Casey et al., "Gender Transformative Approaches to Engaging Men in Gender-Based Violence Prevention: A Review and Conceptual Model," 231–246.

[132] Ibid.

health-related behaviors and addressing biases that may be harmful to women.[133] Based on the effectiveness of group interventions in targeting inner biases by transforming social norms, they present key means of overcoming such inner biases and reducing their negative impact.

Summary

Although inner biases impact the inner workings of the mind, including our decision-making, intuitive judgment, and critical thinking, they can be identified and transformed. However, the process involves targeting not only individuals and personal bias as a source but also engaging the reference group as the foundation of sustaining social norms. As personal bias is shaped by social norms, which are based on cultural biases, transforming social norms and cultural biases serve as the key for overcoming inner biases. In the empirical case of infertility among Arab women in the United States, social behavior changes communication and community discussions present a promising approach to overcoming inner biases associated with women's infertility and transforming health-seeking and support for this population.

---

[133] Cislaghi et al., "Changing Social Norms: The Importance of 'Organized Diffusion' for Scaling Up Community Health Promotion and Wwomen Empowerment Interventions," 936–946.

CHAPTER 5

Bias as Human Nature

Introduction

With the significance of bias established, in this final chapter, I reflect upon the concept of bias as human nature. Within the empirical example presented in chapter 3, we explored together the practical case of bias within the Arab community in the United States, with a focus on fertility. However, bias is not by any means restricted to this instance of infertility or the example reflected in the topic of fertility. In this chapter, I highlight that bias is part of human nature—an issue that is present globally. After reflecting on a few examples of bias, I provide a closing discussion on how such biases can be overcome through both collective and individual efforts.

Bias as Human Nature
Global Examples

In presenting the global examples of bias, it is important again to state the key message from chapter 4—the sources of bias include both personal and cultural sources, which are influenced by societal and cultural stereotypes. I now turn to more general cases of bias that have broader implications for understanding how our inner biases are shaped. Moreover, the purpose is to demonstrate that bias is common; therefore, potential discrimination and other associated consequences of bias are also common.

Because bias influences our decision-making, intuitive judgment, and critical thinking, bias is part of our psychology—whether or not we are consciously aware of our biases. The decision-making and behavior of individuals are shaped by their internalized biases, in some cases, biases that they are unaware of.[134] Due to inner biases, individuals may behave in discriminatory ways without explicit or conscious intent.[135] To demonstrate this reality, I present here real-work examples of bias from recent research: (a) implicit bias and systemic racism, (b) discriminatory nationalism in the context of COVID-19, (c) gender bias, and (d) bias in health care.

Implicit bias and systemic racism

In highlighting implicit bias as automatic mental associations about social groups,[136] Payne and Hannay (2021) posited that the link between implicit bias and systemic racism is a "bias of crowds" as opposed to an individual attitude.[137] Implicit bias is based on the

---

[134] Pritlove et al., "The Good, the Bad, and the Ugly of Implicit Bias," 502–504.

[135] Ibid.

[136] Fazio and Olson, "Implicit Measures in Social Cognition Research: Their Meaning and Use," 297–327; Banaji, "Implicit Attitudes Can Be Measured," 117–150; Petty, Fazio, and Brinol, "The New Implicit Measures: An Overview," 3–18.

[137] Payne and Hannay, "Implicit Bias Reflects Systemic Racism," 927–936; Payne, Vuletich, and Lundberg, "The Bias of Crowds: How Implicit Bias Bridges Personal and Systemic Prejudice," 233–248; Lamont et al., "Bridging

mind's predictions based on the social environment and context of the individual.[138] The concept of implicit bias as a response to the social environment of the individual is consistent with the social and cultural sources of bias that have been presented in chapter 2. Moreover, Payne and Hannay (2021) suggested that implicit bias, if reflected in the social environment and context surrounding an individual, can be used as a marker and driver of systemic inequalities.[139]

Implicit bias is an important indicator because although reported prejudices have been shown to decrease in the last decades,[140] implicit bias has remained,[141] particularly in terms of race and gender. The reason for this discrepancy between implicit bias and expressed prejudice is due not to the elimination of prejudice but to a social change against expressing discriminatory behavior and prejudice.[142] Expanding on this concept, implicit bias and, therefore, the issue of systemic racism exists, at least to an extent, in all environments— whether workplace, city, or country, based on the context of that environment.[143]

In the United States, the most apparent and widespread form of implicit bias can be traced most notably to the history of slavery and further back in history to bias again the indigenous population.

Cultural Sociology and Cognitive Psychology in Three Contemporary Research Programmes," 866–872.

[138] Payne and Hannay, "Implicit Bias Reflects Systemic Racism," 927–936.

[139] Ibid.

[140] Payne and Hannay, "Implicit Bias Reflects Systemic Racism," 927–936; Schuman, Steeh, and Bobo, *Racial Attitudes in America: Trends and Interpretations.*

[141] Hofmann et al., "A Meta-Analysis on the Correlation between the Implicit Association Test and Explicit Self-Report Measures," 1369–1385; Payne and Hannay, "Implicit Bias Reflects Systemic Racism," 927–936; Cameron et al., "Sequential Priming Measures of Implicit Social Cognition: A Meta-Analysis of Associations with Behavior and Explicit Attitudes," 330–350; Nosek et al., "Harvesting Implicit Group Attitudes and Beliefs from a Demonstration Web Site," 101.

[142] Payne and Hannay, "Implicit Bias Reflects Systemic Racism," 927–936.

[143] Payne and Hannay, "Implicit Bias Reflects Systemic Racism," 927–936; Payne, Vuletich, and Lundberg, "The Bias of Crowds: How Implicit Bias Bridges Personal and Systemic Prejudice," 233–248.

Due to the perceptions of Black people and people of color more generally in the United States, a form of pro-White bias has formed, which creates a social source of bias in which those that are non-White are "less than." Stereotypes of people of color reinforce this implicit social bias, which is socially disseminated and shapes the behavior of individuals toward people of color. What is also important about racial bias in the United States is the geographic dispersion, which reinforces the idea that personal bias is influenced by environmental context, as suggested by Payne and Hannay (2021). Confirming this suggestion, an earlier study demonstrated that there is an implicit preference for White as opposed to Black individuals,[144] particularly among older adults.[145] Moreover, there is evidence of disparities based on race in areas such as health and education, which further drives racial inequality.[146]

Although the pro-White implicit bias is described here using the deep-rooted example of the United States, it is globally prevalent, particularly in the context of globalization, which has caused a rise in pro-White sentiments and nationalism in the Western world.[147] These biases are based on negative stereotypes toward non-White social groups, which reinforce the bias against non-White races. For instance, in Sweden, there was proven to be an implicit bias of hiring managers against Arab Muslim job applicants.[148] An example of a

---

[144] Greenwald et al., "Understanding and Using the Implicit Association Test: III. Meta-Analysis of Predictive Validity," 17.

[145] Gonsalkorale, Sherman, and Klauer, "Aging and Prejudice: Diminished Regulation of Automatic Race Bias among Older Adults," 410–414; Nosek, Hawkins, and Frazier, "Implicit Social Cognition: From Measures to Mechanisms," 152–159.

[146] Warikoo et al., "Examining Racial Bias in Education: A New Approach," 508–514; Payne and Hannay, "Implicit Bias Reflects Systemic Racism," 927–936; Orchard, and Price, "County-Level Racial Prejudice and the Black-White Gap in Infant Health Outcomes," 191–198; Leitner et al., "Racial Bias Is Associated with Ingroup Death Rate for Blacks and Whites: Insights from Project Implicit," 220–227.

[147] Anekwe, "Harnessing the Outrage: It's Time the NHS Tackled Racial Bias; Bieber, "Global Nationalism in Times of the COVID-19 Pandemic," 13–25.

[148] Rooth, "Automatic Associations and Discrimination in Hiring: Real World Evidence," 523–534; Nosek, Hawkins, and Frazier, "Implicit Social Cognition:

recent development in bias based in nationalism amid the ongoing COVID-19 pandemic will be presented in the section to follow.

A new source of bias: COVID-19 and the rise of nationalism

With the ongoing COVID-19 pandemic, government responses to prevent the spread of the disease and media coverage of the origins of COVID-19 have resulted in the development of exclusionary nationalism.[149] What is unique about the rise of nationalism during COVID-19 is the concept that due to the global scope of the pandemic, a shared experience was created. In contrast to this shared experience, researchers and observers have noticed an increase in nationalism as a consequence of government responses to the pandemic.[150] The rise of nationalism is not a consequence of developing bias but rather that solidarity and cooperation within each country is necessary in response to the spread of the virus.

The development of nationalism as a source of bias is based on the recent developments in nationalism and exclusionary policies. As described by Bieber (2022), the following global examples are notable examples of bias that have developed in recent years: "These are expressed in a variety of forms, such as the 'America First' platform of US president Donald Trump, the Vote Leave campaign for Brexit, the success of the Hindu nationalism of Narendra Modi, the nationalism promoted by Benjamin Netanyahu in Israel, and the conservative nationalism of Japanese Prime Minister Shinzō Abe."[151] Nationalism presents a form of bias as it results in ethnocentrism in which those outside of the state are viewed as "others," thereby serving as a source of internalized bias against the "others." Nationalism,

---

From Measures to Mechanisms," 152–159.

[149] Bieber, "Global Nationalism in Times of the COVID-19 Pandemic," 13–25.

[150] Bieber, F. (2022). Global nationalism in times of the COVID-19 pandemic. *Nationalities Papers*, *50*(1), 13-25; Rachman, "Nationalism Is a Side Effect of the Coronavirus"; Harari, "The World After Coronavirus"; Tisdall, "Power, Equality, Nationalism: How the Pandemic Will Reshape the World."

[151] Bieber, "Global Nationalism in Times of the COVID-19 Pandemic," 15.

therefore, serves as a social form of bias that can influence inner biases, including implicit bias.

Nationalism is highlighted in this chapter as a form of bias as the global application is visible. Moreover, the impacts, which are reflected in discrimination and hate crimes, are a visible means of understanding the potential and real negative impact of our inner biases. The issue of nationalism results in changes not only in policies, such as immigration policies, but also in the global rise in hate crimes:

> In Germany and the UK hate crimes reported by the police more than doubled between 2014 and 2018; in other countries like the USA, it increased substantially (OSCE ODIHR 2019).[152], [153] The increase appears to be linked to the shift in public discourse and crucial events such as the election of Donald Trump in the USA, the Brexit referendum in the UK, and so-called migration crisis in Europe, which all occurred between 2015 and 2016.[154]

With the rise of nationalism and hate crimes in the foreground of the COVID-19 pandemic, the bias against Chinese and, more broadly, Asian individuals developed due to anti-Chinese and Asian bias corresponding with COVID-19. Although this bias was pres-

---

[152] ODIHR (Office for Democratic Institutions and Human Rights), "Hate Crime Reporting 2018."

[153] "In the United States, between 2014 and 2018, the increase of hate crimes recorded by police from rose from 6,385 to 8,496, in the UK from 52,853 to 111,076, in Germany from 3,059 to 8,113, and in France from 1,662 to 1,838" (Bieber, 2020).

[154] Edwards, and Rushin, "The Effect of President Trump's Election on Hate Crimes"; Cuerden, and Rogers, "Exploring Race Hate Crime Reporting in Wales Following Brexit," 158–164; Rees et al., "Climate of Hate: Similar Correlates of Far Right Electoral Support and Right-Wing Hate Crimes in Germany," 2328; Bieber, "Global Nationalism in Times of the COVID-19 Pandemic," 16.

ent in the United States, the issue was also evident globally (Bieber, 2022):

> Just within two weeks (March 19–April 1, 2020), an online reporting tool in the USA recorded 1,135 cases of COVID-19–related discrimination. Most cases involved verbal assault; others report being denied services, including transport, and being spat on and physically assaulted, usually with direct or indirect reference to COVID-19 (Jeung, 2020). While anti-Chinese and anti-Asian bias have been particularly pronounced in the USA, facilitated by the discursive link made by President Trump, it has been noted elsewhere, including Europe and Australia.[155]

The anti-Chinese and anti-Asian bias was not limited to discrimination against this group. The concept of "otherness" during the COVID-19 pandemic has resulted in bias against additional groups, as presented by Bieber (2022):

> The implicit and explicit link between COVID-19 and the Other has not just been directed against Chinese or Asians; other groups have been blamed for spreading the disease.[156] Hungarian prime minister Viktor Orbán claimed that the spread of the virus was linked to immigration, a central theme of his rhetoric since 2014. Without providing any evidence of the

---

[155] FRA (Fundamental Rights Agency), "Coronavirus Pandemic in the EU—Fundamental Rights Implications"; Escobar, "When Xenophobia Spreads Like a Virus."

[156] OHCHR (Office of the United Nations High Commissioner for Human Rights), *COVID-19 Fears Should Not Be Exploited to Attack and Exclude Minorities — UN Expert.*

link, which appeared implausible, his government closed down the already highly restrictive
asylum system.[157] In the USA, the emergency
rules to combat the pandemic have empowered the Department of Homeland Security to
return illegal and undocumented migrants to
their countries of origin without due process.[158]
In India, officials of the ruling Bharatiya Janata
Party likened Muslims to suicide bombers for
protesting against the new citizenship law, as the
government ordered a lock down and the ruling party and media have singled out Muslims
as "supercarriers."[159] Far-right parties in Europe,
such as the Alternative for Germany (AfD) and
the Austrian Freedom Party (FPÖ), have also
linked the pandemic to the supposed threat of
migration or have demanded repressive measures
specifically aimed at migrants (Jansen, 2020).
In Central Europe, Roma became targets of discrimination, being blamed for spreading the disease (FRA, 2020).

In explaining the reason for the development of such biases,
Bieber (2022) noted the history of linking particular groups, particularly minorities and marginalized communities to disease. By linking
groups to disease, individuals become dehumanized. Moreover, linking groups to disease serves as further "justification" to discriminate
and develop negative biases against such groups. The issue of nationalism during COVID-19, therefore, is a dire example of the source
and development of bias, particularly on the social level. The devel-

---

[157] Inotai, "How Hungary's Orban Blamed Migrants for Coronavirus."

[158] Castellanos-Jankiewicz, "COVID-19 Symposium: US Border Closure Breaches
International Refugee Law."

[159] Daragahi, "Coronavirus Could Be Used by Authoritarian Leaders as Excuse to
Undermine Democracy, Experts Warn"; Kazmin, White, and Palma, "Muslims
Fear Backlash of India's Coronavirus Fury."

opment of such biases, in turn, creates internalized biases, which form into our inner biases. Another ongoing example is the issue of gender bias, which will be presented next.

Gender bias

Gender bias, which is based on judgments, implicit bias, and stereotypes, is common particularly in the professional environment. Researchers have highlighted a global lack of women leaders in politics, business, government, education, nonprofits, and other leadership positions.[160] The reason for the lack of women leaders is due to both conscious and deliberate bias against women,[161] which hinders the advancement of women.[162] For instance, in business, female entrepreneurs and leaders have been found to be disadvantaged in comparison with male entrepreneurs.[163] The disadvantage between men and women is due to a funding gender gap based on underlying biases.[164] Although gender bias in entrepreneurship is a recently explored phenomenon in research, it is reflected in the glass ceiling effect, which has long caused a gap between men and women professionally.[165]

---

[160] Madsen and Andrade, "Unconscious Gender Bias: Implications for Women's Leadership Development," 62–67; Adler, "Women Leaders: Shaping History in the 21st Century," 21–50; Goryunova, Scribner, and Madsen, "The Current Status of Women Leaders Worldwide," 3–23.

[161] Madsen, and Andrade, "Unconscious Gender Bias: Implications for Women's Leadership Development," 62–67.

[162] Ely, Ibarra, and Kolb, "Taking Gender into Account. Theory and Design for Women's Leadership Development Programs," 474–493.

[163] Johnson, Stevenson, and Letwin, "A Woman's Place Is in the…Startup! Crowdfunder Judgments, Implicit Bias, and the Stereotype Content Model," 813–831.

[164] Ibid.

[165] Johnson, Stevenson, and Letwin, "A Woman's Place Is in the…Startup! Crowdfunder Judgments, Implicit Bias, and the Stereotype Content Model," 813–831; Hechavarría et al., "Taking Care of Business: The Impact of Culture and Gender on Entrepreneurs' Blended Value Creation Goals," 225–257; Kanze et al., "We Ask Men to Win and Women Not to Lose: Closing the Gender Gap in Startup Funding," 586-614.

The real gap between men and women is due to gender bias and the proliferation of judgments and stereotypes, which lead to behaviors and decisions against women, based on such biases.[166] Although women are often perceived to be more trustworthy than men, they are disadvantaged in business endeavors due to the perception that business leaders are masculine.[167] The implicit bias of the "masculinity" of leadership and business places women at a disadvantage within society in their careers and in business.[168] Stereotypes, which psychologically reinforce implicit bias,[169] have been determined to be a cause of ongoing gender disparities. Specifically, men have been viewed as stereotypically superior to women in positions of leadership.[170] Based on the ongoing gender gap, researchers have noted that gender disparities may only be eliminated by reducing or eliminating implicit bias.[171] To reduce or eliminate implicit bias, individuals

---

[166] Johnson, Stevenson, and Letwin, "A Woman's Place Is in the…Startup! Crowdfunder Judgments, Implicit Bias, and the Stereotype Content Model," 813–831; Kanze et al., "We Ask Men to Win and Women Not to Lose: Closing the Gender Gap in Startup Funding," 586-614.

[167] Baron, Markman, and Hirsa, "Perceptions of Women and Men as Entrepreneurs: Evidence for Differential Effects of Attributional Augmenting," 923; Johnson, Stevenson, and Letwin, "A Woman's Place Is in the…Startup! Crowdfunder Judgments, Implicit Bias, and the Stereotype Content Model," 813–831; Eagly and Karau, "Role Congruity Theory of Prejudice toward Female Leaders," 573.

[168] Baron, Markman, and Hirsa, "Perceptions of Women and Men as Entrepreneurs: Evidence for Differential Effects of Attributional Augmenting," 923; Eagly and Karau, "Role Congruity Theory of Prejudice toward Female Leaders," 573; Johnson, Stevenson, and Letwin, "A Woman's Place Is in the…Startup! Crowdfunder Judgments, Implicit Bias, and the Stereotype Content Model," 813–831.

[169] Gupta, Turban, and Bhawe, "The Effect of Gender Stereotype Activation on Entrepreneurial Intentions," 1053; Gupta, Goktan, and Gunay, "Gender Differences in Evaluation of New Business Opportunity: A Stereotype Threat Perspective," 273–288.

[170] Madsen and Andrade, "Unconscious Gender Bias: Implications for Women's Leadership Development," 62–67; Ross, *Everyday Bias: Identifying and Navigating Unconscious Judgments in Our Daily Lives.*

[171] Johnson, Stevenson, and Letwin, "A Woman's Place Is in the…Startup! Crowdfunder Judgments, Implicit Bias, and the Stereotype Content Model," 813–831; Barbulescu and Bidwell, "Do Women Choose Different Jobs from

must become aware of their unconscious implicit biases to remove the "invisible barrier" to the advancement of women in the professional setting.[172]

Implicit bias in health care

The real dangers of implicit bias are evident not only in the behaviors of individuals but also in larger societal outcomes—such as in health care. In the health-care profession, both gender bias and racial bias are present, and these issues are not restricted to the United States. In a recent article, Anekwe (2020) presented the outrage surrounding racism in the NHS system within the United Kingdom, which has resulted in a racial health gap and a health gap based on socioeconomic status.[173] Due to the discrimination of individuals based on race and income, individuals are dying prematurely.[174] Moreover, racism and discrimination are associated with poorer mental health and psychological well-being outcomes due to the psychological impact of discrimination on those discriminated against.[175]

The marginalization of individuals due to implicit bias in the health-care environment has resulted in inequitable treatment and poor health outcomes.[176] For example, there is evidence of poorer

---

Men? Mechanisms of Application Segregation in the Market for Managerial Workers," 737–756; Brands and Kilduff, "Just Like a Woman? Effects of Gender-Biased Perceptions of Friendship Network Brokerage on Aattributions and Performance," 1530–1548.

[172] Madsen and Andrade, "Unconscious Gender Bias: Implications for Women's Leadership Development," 62–67.

[173] Anekwe, "Harnessing the Outrage: It's Time the NHS Tackled Racial Bias."

[174] Public Health England, "Local Action on Health Inequalities Understanding and Reducing Ethnic Inequalities in Health"; Barnes et al., "Perceived Discrimination and Mortality in a Population-Based Study of Older Adults," 1241–7; Anekwe, "Harnessing the Outrage: It's Time the NHS Tackled Racial Bias."

[175] Anekwe, "Harnessing the Outrage: It's Time the NHS Tackled Racial Bias."

[176] Sukhera, Watling, and Gonzalez, "Implicit Bias in Health Professions: From Recognition to Transformation," 717–723; Zestcott, Blair, and Stone,

health outcomes in both infant health[177] and overall health outcomes[178] among non-White individuals compared to White individuals in the United States.[179] The poor treatment of marginalized groups is also compounded by disparities on the organizational and systemic levels, which worsens the outcomes for members of such groups.[180] Although implicit biases may influence the behavior of health-care professionals without them being consciously aware of such biases, the behaviors and decisions made based on such implicit biases have a real impact on those served by health-care professionals.[181] With these examples of the negative real-world examples of the impact of bias, we reflect next on how we can overcome bias by taking control.

Overcoming Bias
Taking Control

The key aspect of overcoming bias is identifying the bias and its source and changing the behavior and decision-making that is reflective of the bias. Although implicit bias is evident in numerous global occurrences, implicit bias is enacted in the behavior and decision-making of individuals within society. As introduced previously, because implicit bias is shaped by the environment, when an individual's context changes, their implicit bias may also change.[182] If bias

---

"Examining the Presence, Consequences, and Reduction of Implicit Bias in Health Care: A Narrative Review," 528–542.

[177] Orchard and Price, "County-Level Racial Prejudice and the Black-White Gap in Infant Health Outcomes," 191–198.

[178] Leitner et al., "Racial Bias Is Associated with Ingroup Death Rate for Blacks and Whites: Insights from Project Implicit," 220–227.

[179] Payne and Hannay, "Implicit Bias Reflects Systemic Racism," 927–936.

[180] Sukhera, Watling, and Gonzalez, "Implicit Bias in Health Professions: From Recognition to Transformation," 717–723; Payne and Hannay, "Implicit Bias Reflects Systemic Racism," 927–936.

[181] Sukhera, Watling, and Gonzalez, "Implicit Bias in Health Professions: From Recognition to Transformation," 717–723.

[182] Payne and Hannay, "Implicit Bias Reflects Systemic Racism," 927–936.

can be shaped and even changed by an individual's context, there is an underlying assumption that the implicit bias of the individual can be changed—somehow controlled.

In overcoming bias, the key component is taking control. Taking control involves the recognition that even if we are not consciously aware of our biases, we have responsibility for the actions and behaviors associated with them. Moreover, there is a need to take control over the fact that we have the ability to change our personal biases, even if we have limited control over the social source of bias.

The fact of our control over bias has been reflected in the recent work of Gawronski (2019), who examined implicit bias through cogent science.[183] Contrary to the concept that implicit bias is beyond our control, Gawrsonski (2019) presented evidence that people are mentally aware of their implicit bias.[184] Gawronski (2019) explained that implicit bias is key to understanding social discrimination. Further to explaining that there is a lack of evidence that people are unaware of the mental factors underlying their implicit bias, Gawronski (2019) presented the following properties of implicit bias: (a) conceptual correspondence is central for the interpretation of dissociation between implicit and explicit bias, (b) there is a lack of evidence of unconditional relations between implicit bias and behavior, (c) implicit bias is less stable than explicit bias over time, (d) context is fundamental for the outcomes associated with implicit bias, and (e) implicit bias measurement scores do not provide comprehensive indicators of bias.[185]

Similar to the claim that individuals can become aware of their bias presented by Gawronski (2019), De Houwer (2019) demonstrated that implicit bias can be measured based on the behaviors of individuals.[186] In describing implicit bias, De Houwer (2019) pre-

---

[183] Gawronski, "Six Lessons for a Cogent Science of Implicit Bias and Its Criticism," 574–595.

[184] Ibid.

[185] Gawronski, "Six Lessons for a Cogent Science of Implicit Bias and Its Criticism," 574–595.

[186] De Houwer, "Implicit Bias Is Behavior: A Functional-Cognitive Perspective on Implicit Bias," 835–840.

sented behavioral bias as a behavioral phenomenon that is influenced by cues from the social group to which an individual belongs. In making the link between behavior and implicit bias, De Houwer noted: "Implicit bias is often viewed as a hidden force inside them that makes them perform inappropriate actions."[187]

Because the measurement of implicit bias is not a pure indicator, the outcome of behavior as related to implicit bias is key in understanding how individuals act based on their implicit bias. In fact, the relationship between implicit bias and behavior was determined to be key according to Gawronski (2019), who highlighted the need to ensure a conceptual relation between predictor measures of implicit bias and behavioral criteria, along with a development of more expansive predictor measures for implicit bias.[188] In shifting away from the "uncontrollable" psychological view of implicit bias, De Houwer (2019) presented the concept that implicit bias is a behavioral phenomenon, one that is shaped by social factors (i.e., context).[189] In the view of implicit bias as a behavioral phenomenon, implicit bias is not a mental structure nor something that people possess but is rather something that they do. Moreover, behaviors based on implicit bias provide an indication of the social group to which an individual belongs.[190]

Other researchers, such as Sukhera et al. (2020), have also recommended that implicit bias can be not only recognized but also that interventions such as transformative learning theory (TLT) can be utilized to recognize and manage their implicit biases.[191] In each of the recent arguments presented in recent literature, there is an underlying concept that implicit bias, although involving automated characteristics, results in behavior, which can be controlled. This concept

---

[187] Ibid.

[188] Gawronski, "Six Lessons for a Cogent Science of Implicit Bias and Its Criticism," 574–595.

[189] De Houwer, "Implicit Bias Is Behavior: A Functional-Cognitive Perspective on Implicit Bias," 835–840.

[190] Ibid.

[191] Sukhera, Watling, and Gonzalez, "Implicit Bias in Health Professions: From Recognition to Transformation," 717–723.

is in contrast to the idea that implicit bias is a "hidden mental structure…that is a stable entity is difficult to change and control (e.g., Sukhera et al., 2018)."[192] With evidence that an individual's implicit bias can be made apparent and even measured, I suggest that our inner biases can be recognized by taking control over them.

Perception and Bias
Taking the First Step

With the concept that implicit bias can be controlled, the next question is—*how can we change our inner bias?* In response to this question, I suggest that the first step of taking control over our inner bias is recognizing the negative and positive associations we have established with groups of people, decisions, and actions within their environmental and social context. By recognizing which associations evoke a positive (happiness, laughter, etc.) or negative response (fear, anger, disgust, etc.), we can take the first steps toward controlling our perceptions by reflecting on the biases that have created these perceptions. By taking control over our perceptions, we can begin altering our decisions, behaviors, and intuitive judgments. Taking control, in summary, is the first step in reshaping our inner biases.

The challenge in overcoming bias is that there must be a perceived need to address implicit bias. In other words, an individual with implicit bias must feel a need to take control over the underlying factors that lead to their discriminatory behaviors. This issue was noted by De Houwer (2019) in the statement: "People will only invest effort into trying to prevent or counteract implicit bias only if they perceive it to be potentially inappropriate in some respect."[193] However, individuals may not view their behaviors or implicit bias as inappropriate, particularly if such behaviors are established as part of the social norms within the social group to which they belong. As

---

[192] De Houwer, "Implicit Bias Is Behavior: A Functional-Cognitive Perspective on Implicit Bias," 837.

[193] De Houwer, "Implicit Bias Is Behavior: A Functional-Cognitive Perspective on Implicit Bias," 839.

such, this challenge raises an important need for additional research and practical implications for teaching individuals how to recognize and take control of their inner bias as a means of changing their behavior.

Summary

This chapter serves as the end of this book on our inner biases. We began in chapter 1 with an introduction to the underpinnings of bias and the concept of inner biases. In chapter 2, the cultural and personal sources of biases were presented. In chapter 3, I provided an overview of the empirical case of bias within the Arab community on the topic of fertility. Chapter 4 proposed means of overcoming bias. Finally, in this chapter, I conclude by demonstrating that the consequences of bias are not limited to the case detailed in earlier chapters but can be found in more global phenomena such as inequity, racism, and gender inequality, among others. Therefore, to address the potential consequences of our inner biases, awareness alone is not sufficient. There is a means of controlling our inner biases by recognizing and altering our perceptions to reshape our inner biases. As such, to overcome issues of discrimination and the negative outcomes of behavior associated with implicit bias, we must take control of our inner biases.

REFERENCES

Chapter 1

Baron, J. *Rationality and Intelligence.* New York, NY: Cambridge University Press, 1985.

Baron, J. "The Point of Normative Models in Judgment and Decision Making." *Frontiers in Psychology* 3, (2012): 577. https://doi.org/10.3389/fpsyg.2012.00577

Baron, J. "Normative Models of Judgment and Decision Making." In *Blackwell Handbook of Judgment and Decision Making*, edited by D. J. Koehler and N. Harvey, 19–36. London: Blackwell, 2004.

Bell, D. E., H. Raiffa, and A. Tversky, eds. *Decision Making: Descriptive, Normative, and Prescriptive Interactions.* New York, NY: Cambridge University Press, 1988.

Clarke, J. *Critical Dialogues: Thinking Together in Turbulent Times.* Policy Press, 2019.

Edwards, W., H. Lindman, and L. J. Savage. "Bayesian Statistical Inference for Psychological Research." *Psychology Review* 70, (1963): 193–242.

Ennis, R. H. *Critical Thinking.* Prentice Hall, 1996.

Ennis, R. H., J. Millman, and T. N. Tomko. *Cornell Critical Thinking Tests.* Midwest, 1985.

Facione, P. *California Critical Thinking Skills Test & California Critical Thinking Dispositions Inventory.* California Academic Press, 1992.

Facione, P. *Critical Thinking: What It Is and Why It Counts*. California Academic Press, 2007.
http://www.insightassessment.com/pdf_files/DEXadobe.PDF

Fischhoff, B. "Judgment and Decision Making." *WIREs Cognitive Science* 1, no. 5 (2010): 724–735.
https://doi.org/10.1002/wcs.65

Freeling, A. N. S. "A Philosophical Basis for Decision Aiding." *Theory Decision* 16, (1984): 179–206.

Friedman, S. H. "Culture, Bias, and Understanding: We Can Do Better." *The Journal of the American Academy of Psychiatry and the Law* 45, (2017): 166–139.

Hart, S. "Adaptive Heuristics." *Econometrica* 73, no. 5 (2005): 1401–1430.

Hebl, M. R. and J. F. Dovidio. "Promoting the 'Social' in the Examination of Social Stigmas." *Personality and Social Psychology Review* 9, no. 2 (2005): 156–182.

Kahneman, D., P. Slovic, and A. Tversky. *Judgment Under Uncertainty: Heuristics and Biases*. Cambridge University Press, 1982.

Kyburg, H. E. and H. E. Smokler, eds. *Studies in Subjective Probability*. Wiley, 1964.

Mccullagh, C. B. "Bias in Historical Description, Interpretation, and Explanation." *History and Theory 39, no.* 1 (2002): 39–66.
https://doi.org/10.1111/0018-2656.00112

Mega, L. F., G. Gigerenzer, and K. G. Volz. "Do Intuitive and Deliberate Judgments Rely on Two Distinct Neural Systems? A Case Study in Face Processing." *Frontiers in Human Neuroscience*, (2015). https://doi.org/10.3389/fnhum.2015.00456

Norris, S. P. and R. H. Ennis. *Evaluating Critical Thinking*. Midwest, 1989.

Schwarz, N. "Social Judgment and Attitudes: Warmer, More Social, and Less Conscious." *European Journal of Social Psychology 30*, (2000): 149–176.

Sherif, M., C. Sherif, and R. Nebergall. *Attitude and Attitude Change: The Social Judgment-Involvement Approach*. W. B. Saunders, 1965.

Solso, R. L., M. K. MacLin, and O. H. MacLin. *Cognitive Psychology*. Pearson Education New Zealand, 2005.

VandenBos, G. R., ed. (2007). "Intuitive Judgment." *APA Dictionary of Psychology*, (2007).

Volz, K. G. and T. Zander. "Primed for Intuition?" *Neuroscience of Decision Making* 1, (2014): 26–34. https://doi.org/10.2478/ndm-2014-0001

Watson, G. and E. M. Glaser. *Watson-Glaser Critical Thinking Appraisal*. Psychological Corp, 1980.

West, R. F., K. E. Stanovich, and M. E. Toplak. "Heuristics and Biases as Measures of Critical Thinking: Associations with Cognitive Ability and Thinking Dispositions." *Journal of Educational Psychology* 100, no. 4 (2008): 930–941. https://doi.org/10.1037/a0012842

Yingst, T. E. "Cultural Bias." In *Encyclopedia of Child Behavior and Development, edited by* S. Goldstein and J. A. Naglieri. Springer, 2011. https://doi.org/10.1007/978-0-387-79061-9_749

Chapter 2

Baron, J. "Thinking About Consequences." *Journal of Moral Education* 19, (1990): 77–87.

Baron, J. "Nonconsequentialist Decisions (with Commentary and Reply)." *Behavioral and Brain Sciences* 17, (1994): 1–42.

Baron, J. "Normative Models of Judgment and Decision Making." In *Blackwell Handbook of Judgment and Decision Making*, edited by D. J. Koehler and N. Harvey, 19–36. London: Blackwell, 2004.

Baron, J. *Thinking and Deciding, 4th Ed*. New York, NY: Cambridge University Press, 2008.

Bell, D. E., H. Raiffa, and A. Tversky, eds. *Decision Making: Descriptive, Normative, and Prescriptive Interactions*. New York, NY: Cambridge University Press, 1988.

Best, J. B. *Cognitive Psychology*. West Publishing Co, 1986.

Erbe, N. *Conflict Case Studies*. UC San Diego, 2019.

https://escholarship.org/uc/item/40t6z9x0

Fischhoff, B. "Judgment and Decision Making." *WIREs Cognitive Science* 1, no. 5 (2010): 724–735. https://doi.org/10.1002/wcs.65

Freeling, A. N. S. "A Philosophical Basis for Decision Aiding." *Theory of Decision* 16, (1984): 179–206.

Friedman, S. H. "Culture, Bias, and Understanding: We Can Do Better." *The Journal of the American Academy of Psychiatry and the Law* 45, (2017): 166–139.

Gigerenzer, G. "Why Heuristics Work." *Perspectives on Psychological Science 3, no.* 1 (2008): 20–29.

Haddad, A., R. Doherty, and R. Purtilo. "Chapter 5—Respect in a Diverse Society." In *Health Professional and Patient Interaction*, (2019). https://doi.org/10.1016/B978-0-323-53362-1.00005-0

Hansen, K., M. Gerbasi, A. Todorov, E. Kruse, and E. Pronin. "People Claim Objectivity After Knowingly Using Biased Strategies." *Personality and Social Psychology Bulletin* 40, no. 6 (2014): 691–699.

Hart, S. "Adaptive Heuristics." *Econometrica* 73, no. 5 (2005): 1401–1430.

Hebl, M. R. and J. F. Dovidio. "Promoting the 'Ssocial' in the Examination of Social Stigmas." *Personality and Social Psychology Review* 9, no. 2 (2005): 156–182.

Kahneman, D., P. Slovic, and A. Tversky. *Judgment Under Uncertainty: Heuristics and Biases.* Cambridge University Press, 1982.

Kerr, N. L., R. J. MacCoun, and G. P. Kramer. "Bias in Judgment: Comparing Individuals and Groups." *Psychological Review* 103, no. 4 (1996): 687.

Kirmayer, L. J., C. Rousseau, and M. Lashley. "The Place of Culture in Forensic Psychiatry." Journal-American Academy of Psychiatry and the Law 35, no. 1 (2007): 98.

Koehler, D. J. and N. Harvey. *Blackwell Handbook of Judgment and Decision Making.* Blackwell Publishing, 2004.

Konow, J. "Blind Spots: The Effects of Information and Stakes on Fairness Bias and Dispersion." *Social Justice Research* 18, no. 4 (2005): 349–390.

Kyburg, H. E. and H. E. Smokler, eds. *Studies in Subjective Probability.* Wiley, 1964.

Larrick, R. P. "Debiasing." In *Blackwell Handbook of Judgment and Decision Making*, edited by D. J. Koehler and N. Harvey, 316–337. London: Blackwell, 2004.

Mccullagh, C. B. "Bias in Historical Description, Interpretation, and Explanation." *History and Theory* 39, no. 1 (2002): 39–66. https://doi.org/10.1111/0018-2656.00112

Medin, D. L. and B. H. Ross. *Cognitive Psychology.* Harcourt Brace Jovanovich, 1992.

Michalewicz, Z. and D. B. Fogel. *How to Solve It: Modern Heuristics.* Springer Science & Business Media, 2013.

Perry, S. P., M. C. Murphy, M. C., and J. F. Dovidio, J. F. "Modern Prejudice: Subtle, but Unconscious? The Role of Bias Awareness in Whites' Perceptions of Personal and Others' Biases." *Journal of Experimental Social Psychology* 61, (2015): 64–78.

Pronin, E. "Perception and Misperception of Bias in Human Judgment." *Trends in Cognitive Sciences* 11, no. 1 (2007): 37–43.

Sagiv, M. (2015). "*Cultural Bias in Judicial Decision Making.*" Boston College Journal of Law & Social Justice, (2015): 35, 229. http://lawdigitalcommons.bc.edu/jlsj/vol35/iss2/3

Schwarz, N. "Social Judgment and Attitudes: Warmer, More Social, and Less Conscious." *European Journal of Social Psychology* 30, (2000): 149–176.

Solso, R. L., M. K. MacLin, and O. H. MacLin. *Cognitive Psychology.* Pearson Education New Zealand, 2005.

Volz, K. G. and T. Zander. "Primed for Intuition?" *Neuroscience of Decision Making* 1, (2014): 26–34. https://doi.org/10.2478/ndm-2014-0001

Waldmann, M. R., J. Nagel, and A. Wiegmann. "Moral Judgment." (2012).

West, R. F., K. E. Stanovich, and M. E. Toplak. "Heuristics and Biases as Measures of Critical Thinking: Associations with Cognitive

Ability and Thinking Dispositions." *Journal of Educational Psychology* 100, no. 4 (2008): 930–941. https://doi.org/10.1037/a0012842

Wood, J. T. *Gender, Communication and Culture, Intercultural Communication.* 2000; see also Wall, V. D. and M. L. Dewhurst. *Mediator Gender: Communication Differences in Resolved and Unresolved Mediations.* 1985; Weingarten, H. R. and E. Douvan. "Male and Female Visions of Mediation." *Negotiation Journal* 4, (1985): 349–358.

Yingst, T. E. "Cultural Bias." In *Encyclopedia of Child Behavior and Development*, edited by S. Goldstein and J. A. Naglieri. Springer, 2011. https://doi.org/10.1007/978-0-387-79061-9_749.

Chapter 3

Ali, S., R. Sophie, A. M. Imam, F. I. Khan, S. F. Ali, A. Shaikh, and S. Farid-ul-Hasnain. "Knowledge, Perceptions and Myths regarding Infertility among Selected Adult Population in Pakistan: A Cross-Sectional Study." *BMC Public Health* 11, no. 1 (2011): 1–7.

Ali, B. H., A. Ziada, I. Al Husseni, S. Beegam, B. Al-Ruqaishi, and A. Nemmar. "Effect of Acacia Gum on Blood Pressure in Rats with Adenine-Induced Chronic Renal Failure." *Phytomedicine* 18, no. 13 (2011): 1176–1180.

Amini, L., B. Ghorbani, and B. Afshar. "The Comparison of Infertility Stress and Perceived Social Support in Infertile Women and Spouses of Infertile Men." *Iran Journal of Nursing* 32, no. 122 (2020): 74–85. https://doi.org/10.29252/ijn.32.122.80

Balen, A. H. *Infertility in Practice.* CRC Press, 2014.

Bell, K. "Constructions of 'Infertility' and Some Lived Experiences of Involuntary Childlessness." *Affilia* 28, no. 3 (2013): 284–295. https://doi.org/10.1177/0886109913495726

Benyamini, Y., M. Gozlan, and A. Weissman. "Normalization as a Strategy for Maintaining Quality of Life while Coping with

Infertility in a Pronatalist Culture." *International Journal of Behavioral Medicine* 24, no. 6 (2017): 871–879. https://doi.org/10.1007/s12529-017-9656-1

Berger, R., M. S. Paul, and L. A. Henshaw. "Women's Experience of Infertility: A Multi-Systemic Perspective." *Journal of International Women's Studies* 14, no. 1 (2013): 54–68.

Berghuis, J. P. and A. L. Stanton. "Adjustment to a Dyadic Stressor: A Longitudinal Study of Coping and Depressive Symptoms in Infertile Couples over an Insemination Attempt." *Journal of Consulting and Clinical Psychology* 70, no. 2 (2002): 433–438. http://dx.doi.org/10.1037/0022-006X.70.2.433

Boivin, J., L. Bunting, J. A. Collins, and K. G. Nygren. "International Estimates of Infertility Prevalence and Treatment-Seeking: Potential Need and Demand for Infertility Medical Care." *Human Reproduction* 22, no. 6 *(Oxford, England, 2007)*: 1506–1512.

https://doi.org/10.1093/humrep/dem046

Burns, L. H., S. N. Covington, and R. D. Kempers. *Infertility Counseling*. Cambridge University Press, 2006.

Crabtree, S. A. "Culture, Gender and the Influence of Social Change amongst Emirati Families in the United Arab Emirates." *Journal of Comparative Family Studies* 38, no. 4 (2007): 575–588.

Carter, J., L. Applegarth, L. Josephs, E. Grill, R. E. Baser, and Z. Rosenwaks, Z. "A Cross-Sectional Cohort Study of Infertile Women Awaiting Oocyte Donation: The Emotional, Sexual, and Quality-of-Life Impact." *Fertility and Sterility* 95, no. 2 (2011): 711–716.

Centers for Disease Control and Prevention (CDC). "Infertility." *Key Statistics from the National Survey of Family Growth - I Listing*, (2019).

https://www.cdc.gov/nchs/nsfg/key_statistics/i_2015-2017.htm#infertility

Cousineau, T. M. and A. D. Domar. "Psychological Impact of Infertility." *Best Practice & Research Clinical Obstetrics & Gynaecology* 21, no. 2 (2007): 293–308. https://doi.org/10.1016/j.bpobgyn.2006.12.003

de Kok, B. "Infertility in Malawi: Exploring Its Impact and Social Consequences, (2008).

Deribe, K., A. Anberbir, G. Regassa, T. Belachew, and S. Biadgilign. "Infertility Perceived Causes and Experiences in Rural South West Ethiopia." *Ethiop J Health Sci* 17, no. 2 (2007).

Dierickx, S. "'With the Kanyaleng and the Help of God, You Don't Feel Ashamed': Women Experiencing Infertility in Casamance, Senegal." *Culture, Health & Sexuality*, (2020): 1–16. https://doi.org/10.1080/13691058.2020.1833366

Dyer, S. J., N. Abrahams, M. Hoffman, and Z. M. van der Spuy. "'Men Leave Me as I Cannot Have Children': Women's Experiences with Involuntary Childlessness." *Human Reproduction* 17, no. 6 (2002): 1663–1668.

Dyer, S. J., N. Abrahams, N. E. Mokoena, and Z. M. van der Spuy. "'You Are a Man because You Have Children': Experiences, Reproductive Health Knowledge and Treatment-Seeking Behaviour among Men Suffering from Couple Infertility in South Africa." *Human Reproduction* 19, no. 4 (2004): 960–967.

Dyer, S., C. Lombard, and Z. van der Spuy. "Psychological Distress among Men Suffering from Couple Infertility in South Africa: A Quantitative Assessment." *Human Reproduction* 24, no. 11 (2009): 2821–2826.

Gonzalez, L. O. "Infertility as a Transformational Process: A Framework for Psychotherapeutic Support of Infertile Women." *Issues in Mental Health Nursing* 21, (2000): 619–633.

Greil, A. L., J. McQuillan, and K. Slauson-Blevins. "The Social Construction of Infertility." *Sociology Compass* 5, no. 8 (2011): 736–746.

Greil, A. L., K. Slauson-Blevins, and J. McQuillan. "The Experience of Infertility: A Review of Recent Literature." *Sociology of Health & Illness* 32, no. 1 (2010): 140–162. https://doi.org/10.1111/j.1467-9566.2009.01213.x

Gurunath, S., Z. Pandian, R. A. Anderson, and S. Bhattacharya. "Defining Infertility—A Systematic Review of Prevalence Studies." *Human Reproduction Update* 17, no. 5 (2011): 575–588.

Henry, H. M., W. B. Stiles, M. W. Biran, and S. Hinkle. "Perceived Parental Acculturation Behaviors and Control as Predictors of Subjective Well-Being in Arab American College Students." *The Family Journal* 16, no. 1 (2008): 28–34.

Höbek Akarsu, R. and N. Kızılkaya Beji. "Spiritual and Religious Issues of Stigmatization Women with Infertility: A Qualitative Study." *Journal of Religion and Health* 60, no. 1 (2021): 256–267. https://doi.org/10.1007/s10943-019-00884-w

Hollos, M., U. Larsen, O. Obono, and B. Whitehouse. "The Problem of Infertility in High Fertility Populations: Meanings, Consequences and Coping Mechanisms in Two Nigerian Communities." *Social Science & Medicine* 68, no. 11 (2009): 2061–2068. https://doi.org/10.1016/j.socscimed.2009.03.008

Ibrahim, M. M., S. A. A. Rahman Al Awar, N. D. Nayeri, M. Al-Jefout, F. Ranjbar, and Z. B. Moghadam. "Perceptions of Infertility among Women in United Arab Emirates: A Qualitative Study." *Electronic Physician* 11, no. 2 (2019). http://dx.doi.org/10.19082/7544

Inhorn, M. C. *Infertility and Patriarchy: The Cultural Politics of Gender and Family Life in Egypt.* University of Pennsylvania Press, 1996.

Inhorn, M. C. "'The Worms Are Weak' Male Infertility and Patriarchal Paradoxes in Egypt." *Men and Masculinities* 5, no. 3 (2003): 236–256.

Inhorn, M. and F. Van Balen, eds. *Infertility Around the Globe: New Thinking on Childlessness, Gender, and Reproductive Technologies.* University of California Press, 2002.

Kimani, V. and J. Olenja. "Infertility: Cultural Dimensions and Impact on Women in Selected Communities in Kenya." *African Anthropologist* 8, no. 2 (2001): 200–214.

Macer, M. L. and H. S. Taylor. "Endometriosis and Infertility: A Review of the Pathogenesis and Treatment of Endometriosis-Associated Infertility." *Obstetrics and Gynecology Clinics* 39, no. 4 (2012): 535–549.

Martins, M. V., B. D. Peterson, V. M. Almeida, and M. E. Costa. "Direct and Indirect Effects of Perceived Social Support on Women's Infertility-Related Stress." *Human Reproduction* 26, no. 8 (2011): 2113–2121.
https://doi.org/10.1093/humrep/der157

Mascarenhas, M. N., S. R. Flaxman, T. Boerma, S. Vanderpoel, and G. A. Stevens. "National, Regional, and Global Trends in Infertility Prevalence Since 1990: A Systematic Aanalysis of 277 Health Surveys." *PLoS Medicine* 9, no. 12 (2012).
https://doi.org/10.1371/journal.pmed.1001356

Mete, S., S. Fata, and M. Aluş Tokat. "Feelings, Opinions and Experiences of Turkish Women with Infertility: A Qualitative Study." *Health Informatics Journal* 26, no. 1 (2020): 528–538.
https://doi.org/10.1177%2F1460458219839628

Moghaddam, S., C. Yang, M. Rekharsky, Y. H. Ko, K. Kim, Y. Inoue, and M. K. Gilson. (2011). "New Ultrahigh Affinity Host—Guest Complexes of Cucurbit [7] Uril with Bicyclo [2.2. 2] Octane and Adamantane Guests: Thermodynamic Analysis and Evaluation of m2 Affinity Calculations." *Journal of the American Chemical Society* 133, no. 10 (2011): 3570–3581.

Montazeri, A. "Infertility and Health-Related Quality of Life: Minireview of the Literature." *Journal of Family and Reproductive Health*, (2007): 55–58.

Ombelet W. "Global Access to Infertility Care in Developing Countries: A Case of Human Rights, Equity and Social Justice." *Facts, Views & Vision in ObGyn* 3, no. 4 (2011): 257–266.
https://www.ncbi.nlm.nih.gov/pmc/articles/PMC3987469/

Pennings, G. and H. Mertes. "Ethical Issues in Infertility Treatment." *Best Practice & Research Clinical Obstetrics & Gynaecology* 26, no. 6 (2012): 853–863.
https://doi.org/10.1016/j.bpobgyn.2012.04.002

Peterson, B. D., C. R. Newton, K. H. Rosen, and R. S. Schulman. "Coping Processes of Couples Experiencing Infertility." *Family Relations* 55, no. 2 (2006): 227–239.

Rutstein, S. O. and I. H. Shah. *Infecundity, Infertility, and Childlessness in Developing Countries* (No. 9). ORC Macro, MEASURE DHS, 2004.

Satheesan, S. C. and V. A. Satyanarayana. "Quality of Marital Relationship, Partner Violence, Psychological Distress, and Resilience in Women with Primary Infertility." *International Journal of Community Medicine and Public Health* 5, no. 2 (2018): 734–739.

http://dx.doi.org/10.18203/2394-6040.ijcmph20180259

Schmid, J., S. Kirchengast, E. Vytiska-Binstorfer, and J. Huber. "Infertility Caused by PCOS—Health-Related Quality of Life among Austrian and Moslem Immigrant Women in Austria." *Human Reproduction* 19, no. 10 (2004): 2251–2257.

https://doi.org/10.1093/humrep/deh432

Sormunen, T., A. Aanesen, B. Fossum, K. Karlgren, and M. Westerbotn. "Infertility-Related Communication and Coping Strategies among Women Affected by Primary or Secondary Infertility." *Journal of Clinical Nursing* 27, nos. 1–2 (2018): e335–e344.

https://doi.org/10.1111/jocn.13953

Sudha, G. and K. S. N. Reddy. "Causes of Female Infertility: A Cross-Sectional Study." *International Journal of Latest Research in Science and Technology* 2, no. 6 (2013): 119–123.

Vitale, S. G., V. L. La Rosa, A. M. C. Rapisarda, and A. S. Lagana. "Psychology of Infertility and Assisted Reproductive Treatment: The Italian Situation." *Journal of Psychosomatic Obstetrics & Gynecology* 38, no. 1 (2017): 1–3.

https://doi.org/10.1080/0167482X.2016.1244184

Volgsten, H., A. S. Svanberg, L. Ekselius, Ö. Lundkvist, and I. S. Poromaa. "Risk Factors for Psychiatric Disorders in Infertile Women and Men Undergoing In Vitro Fertilization Treatment." *Fertility and Sterility* 93, no. 4 (2010): 1088–1096.

World Health Organization (WHO). "Infertility Is a Global Public Health Issues." *Sexual and Reproductive Health*, (2021).

https://www.who.int/reproductivehealth/topics/infertility/perspective/en/

World Health Organization (WHO). *International Classification of Diseases, 11th Revision (ICD-11)*. WHO, 2018.

Yüksekol, Ö. D., M. Duman, and Y. D. Ozan. "The Relationship between Gender Perception Levels and Infertility Distress of Infertile Women." *Journal of Health Research*, (2020). https://doi.org/10.1108/JHR-04-2020-0088

Zayed, A. A. and M. A. El-Hadidy. "Sexual Satisfaction and Self-Esteem in Women with Primary Infertility." *Middle East Fertility Society Journal 25, no.* 1 (2020): 1–5. https://doi.org/10.1186/s43043-020-00024-5

Ziegler, D., B. Borghese, and C. Chapron. "Endometriosis and Infertility: Pathophysiology and Management." *The Lancet 376, no.* 9742 (2010): 730–738. https://doi.org/10.1016/S0140-6736(10)60490-4

Hess, R. F., R. Ross, J. L. Gililland. "Infertility, Psychological Distress, and Coping Strategies among Women in Mali, West Africa: A Mixed-Methods Study." *African Journal of Reproductive Health* 22, no. 1 (2018): 60–72.

Ozturk, R., A. Taner, S. E. Guneri, and B. Yilmaz. "Another Face of Violence Aagainst Women: Infertility." *Pakistan Journal of Medical Sciences* 33, no. 4 (2017): 909.

Roushangar, D. M. "America's Arab Refugees: Vulnerability and Health on the Margins," edited by Marcia C. Inhorn. *Journal of Refugee Studies*, (2021).

Webair, H. H., T. A. T. Ismail, S. B. Ismail, and A. J. Khaffaji. "Patient-Centred Infertility Care among Arab Women Experiencing Infertility: A Qualitative Study." *BMJ Open* 11, no. 6 (2021).

Chapter 4

Ali, S., R. Sophie, A. M. Imam, F. I. Khan, S. F. Ali, A. Shaikh, and S. Farid-ul-Hasnain. "Knowledge, Perceptions and Myths regarding Infertility among Selected Adult Population in Pakistan: A Cross-Sectional Study." *BMC Public Health* 11, no. 1 (2011): 1–7.

Bell, D. C. and M. L. Cox. "Social Norms: Do We Love Norms Too Much?" *Journal of Family Theory & Review* 7, no. 1 (2015): 28–46.

Boivin, J., L. Bunting, J. A. Collins, and K. G. Nygren. "International Estimates of Infertility Prevalence and Treatment-Seeking: Potential Nneed and Demand for Infertility Medical Care." *Human Reproduction* 22, no. 6 (2007): 1506–1512. https://doi.org/10.1093/humrep/dem046

Carter, J., L. Applegarth, L. Josephs, E. Grill, R. E. Baser, and Z. Rosenwaks. "A Cross-Sectional Cohort Study of Infertile Women Awaiting Oocyte Donation: The Emotional, Sexual, and Quality-of-Life Impact." *Fertility and Sterility* 95, no. 2 (2011): 711–716.

Casey, E., J. Carlson, S. Two Bulls, and A. Yager. "Gender Transformative Approaches to Engaging Men in Gender-Based Violence Prevention: A Review and Conceptual Model." *Trauma, Violence, & Abuse* 19, no. 2 (2018): 231–246.

Cislaghi, B., E. K. Denny, M. Cissé, P. Gueye, B. Shrestha, P. N. Shrestha, and C. J. Clark. "Changing Social Norms: The Importance of 'Organized Diffusion' for Scaling Up Community Health Promotion and Women Empowerment Interventions." *Prevention Science* 20, no. 6 (2019): 936–946.

Crooks, C. V., P. Jaffe, C. Dunlop, A. Kerry, and D. Exner-Cortens. "Preventing Gender-Based Violence among Adolescents and Young Adults: Lessons from 25 Years of Program Development and Evaluation." *Violence against Women* 25, no. 1 (2019): 29–55.

Ennis, R. H. *Critical Thinking.* Prentice Hall, 1996.

Ennis, R. H., J. Millman, and T. N. Tomko. *Cornell Critical Thinking Tests.* Midwest, 1985.

Facione, P. *California Critical Thinking Skills Test & California Critical Thinking Dispositions Inventory.* California Academic Press, 1992.

Facione, P. *Critical Thinking: What It Is and Why It Counts.* California Academic Press, 2007. http://www.insightassessment.com/pdf_files/DEXadobe.PDF

Gelfand, M. J. and J. C. Jackson. "From One Mind to Many: The Emerging Science of Cultural Norms." *Current Opinion in Psychology* 8, (2016): 175–181.

Greil, A. L., J. McQuillan, and K. Slauson-Blevins. "The Social Construction of Infertility." *Sociology Compass* 5, no. 8 (2011): 736–746.

Gurunath, S., Z. Pandian, R. A. Anderson, and S. Bhattacharya. "Defining Infertility—A Systematic Review of Prevalence Studies." *Human Reproduction Update* 17, no. 5 (2011): 575–588.

Inhorn, M. C. "'The Worms Are Weak' Male Infertility and Patriarchal Paradoxes in Egypt." *Men and Masculinities* 5, no. 3 (2003): 236–256.

Kumar, V., A. Kumar, A. K. Ghosh, R. Samphel, R. Yadav, D. Yeung, and G. L. Darmstadt. "Enculturating Science: Community-Centric Design of Behavior Change Interactions for Accelerating Health Impact." *Seminars in Perinatology* 39, (2015): 393–415.

Linos, N., N. Slopen, S. V. Subramanian, L. Berkman, and I. Kawachi. "Influence of Community Social Norms on Spousal Violence: A Population-Based Multilevel Study of Nigerian Women." *American Journal of Public Health* 103, no. 1 (2013): 148–155.

Mackie, G., F. Moneti, H. Shakya, and E. Denny. *What Are Social Norms? How Are They Measured?* New York: UNICEF and UCSD, 2015.

Mccullagh, C. B. "Bias in Historical Description, Interpretation, and Explanation." *History and Theory* 39, no. 1 (2002): 39–66. https://doi.org/10.1111/0018-2656.00112

Miller, D. T. and D. A. Prentice. "Changing Norms to Change Behavior." *Annual Review of Psychology* 67, (2016): 339–361.

Montazeri, A. "Infertility and Health-Related Quality of LifeM mini-review of the Literature." *Journal of Family and Reproductive Health*, (2007): 55–58.

Norris, S. P. and R. H. Ennis. *Evaluating Critical Thinking*. Midwest, 1989.

Roy, S., M. Hidrobo, J. Hoddinott, and A. Ahmed. "Transfers, Behavior Change Communication, and Intimate Partner Violence: Postprogram Evidence from Rural Bangladesh." *Review of Economics and Statistics* 101, no. 5 (2019): 865–877.

Saxena, D. P. "The 'Reference Group' Concept." *Social Science* 46, no. 3 (1971): 155–164.

Schmid, J., S. Kirchengast, E. Vytiska-Binstorfer, and J. Huber. "Infertility Caused by PCOS—Health-Related Quality of Life among Austrian and Moslem Immigrant Women in Austria." *Human Reproduction* 19, no. 10 (2004): 2251–2257. https://doi.org/10.1093/humrep/deh432

Solso, R. L., M. K. MacLin, and O. H. MacLin. *Cognitive Psychology.* Pearson Education New Zealand, 2005.

Suzor, N., M. Dragiewicz, B. Harris, R. Gillett, J. Burgess, and T. Van Geelen. "Human Rights by Design: The Responsibilities of Social Media Platforms to Address Gender-Based Violence Online." *Policy & Internet* 11, no. 1 (2019): 84–103.

West, R. F., K. E. Stanovich, and M. E. Toplak. "Heuristics and Biases as Measures of Critical Thinking: Associations with Cognitive Ability and Thinking Dispositions." *Journal of Educational Psychology* 100, no. 4 (2008): 930–941. https://doi.org/10.1037/a0012842

World Health Organization (WHO). *International Classification of Diseases, 11th Revision (ICD-11).* WHO, 2018.

World Health Organization (WHO). "Infertility Is a Global Public Health Issues." *Sexual and Reproductive Health,* (2021). https://www.who.int/reproductivehealth/topics/infertility/perspective/en/

Ziegler, D., B. Borghese, and C. Chapron. "Endometriosis and Infertility: Pathophysiology and Management." *The Lancet* 376, no. 9742 (2010): 730–738. https://doi.org/10.1016/S0140-6736(10)60490-4

Chapter 5

Adler, N. J. "Women Leaders: Shaping History in the 21st Century." In *Women as Global Leaders,* edited by F. W. Ngunjiri and S. R. Madsen, 21–50. Information Age Publishing, 2015.

Anekwe, L. "Harnessing the Outrage: It's Time the NHS Tackled Racial Bias. *British Medical Journal* 368, (2020).

Banaji, M. R. "Implicit Attitudes Can Be Measured." *The Nature of Remembering: Essays in Honor of Robert G. Crowder*, (2001): 117–150.

Barbulescu, R. and M. Bidwell. "Do Women Choose Different Jobs from Men? Mechanisms of Application Segregation in the Market for Managerial Workers." *Organization Science* 24, no. 3 (2013): 737–756.

Baron, R. A., G. D. Markman, and A. Hirsa. "Perceptions of Women and Men as Entrepreneurs: Evidence for Differential Effects of Attributional Augmenting." *Journal of Applied psychology* 86, no. 5 (2001): 923.

Bieber, F. "Global Nationalism in Times of the COVID-19 Pandemic." *Nationalities Papers* 50, no. 1 (2022): 13–25.

Brands, R. A. and M. Kilduff. "Just Like a Woman? Effects of Gender-Biased Perceptions of Friendship Network Brokerage on Attributions and Performance." *Organization Science* 25, no. 5 (2014): 1530–1548.

Brownstein, M., A. Madva, and B. Gawronski. "Understanding Implicit Bias: Putting the Criticism into Perspective." *Pacific Philosophical Quarterly* 101, no. 2 (2020): 276–307.

Cameron, C. D., J. L. Brown-Iannuzzi, and B. K. Payne. "Sequential Priming Measures of Implicit Social Cognition: A Meta-Analysis of Associations with Behavior and Explicit Attitudes." *Personality and Social Psychology Review* 16, no. 4 (2012): 330–350.

De Houwer, J. "Implicit Bias Is Behavior: A Functional-Cognitive Perspective on Implicit Bias." *Perspectives on Psychological Science* 14, no. 5 (2019): 835–840.

Eagly, A. H. and S. J. Karau. "Role Congruity Theory of Prejudice toward Female Leaders." *Psychological Review* 109, no. 3 (2002): 573.

Ely, R. J., H. Ibarra, and D. Kolb. "Taking Gender into Account. Theory and Design for Women's Leadership Development Programs." *Academy of Management Learning and Education* 10, no. 3 (2011): 474–493. https://doi.org/10.5465/amle.2010.0046

Fazio, R. H. and M. A. Olson. "Implicit Measures in Social Cognition Research: Their Meaning and Use." *Annual Review of Psychology* 54, no. 1 (2003): 297–327.

Gawronski, B. "Six Lessons for a Cogent Science of Implicit Bias and its Criticism." *Perspectives on Psychological Science* 14, no. 4 (2019): 574–595.

Gawronski, B. and J. De Houwer. "Implicit Measures in Social and Personality Psychology." In *Handbook of Research Methods in Social and Personality Psychology*, 2nd Edition, edited by H. T. Reis and C. M. Judd. Cambridge University Press, 2014.

Goryunova, E., R. T. Scribner, and S. R. Madsen. "The Current Status of Women Leaders Wworldwide." In *Handbook of Research on Gender and Leadership*, edited by S. R. Madsen, 3–23. Edward Elgar Publishing, 2017.

Greenwald, A. G. and C. K. Lai. "Implicit Social Coognition." *Annual Review of Psychology* 71, (2020): 419–445.

Greenwald, A. G., T. A. Poehlman, E. L. Uhlmann, and M. R. Banaji. "Understanding and Using the Implicit Association Test: III. Meta-Analysis of Predictive Validity." *Journal of Personality and Social Psychology* 97, no. 1 (2009): 17.

Gupta, V. K., D. B. Turban, and N. M. Bhawe. "The Effect of Gender Stereotype Activation on Entrepreneurial Intentions." *Journal of Applied Psychology* 93, no. 5 (2008): 1053.

Gupta, V. K., A. B. Goktan, and G. Gunay. "Gender Differences in Evaluation of New Business Opportunity: A Stereotype Threat Perspective." *Journal of Business Venturing* 29, no. 2 (2014): 273–288.

Harari, Y. N. "The World After Coronavirus." *Financial Times,* (2020). https://www.ft.com/content/19d90308-6858-11ea-a3c9-1fe6fed-cca75

Hechavarría, D. M., S. A. Terjesen, A. E. Ingram, M. Renko, R. Justo, and A. Elam. "Taking Care of Business: The Impact of Culture and Gender on Entrepreneurs' Blended Value Creation Goals." *Small Business Economics* 48, no. 1 (2017): 225–257.

Hofmann, W., B. Gawronski, T. Gschwendner, H. Le, and M. Schmitt. "A Meta-Analysis on the Correlation between the Implicit Association Test and Explicit Self-Report Measures." *Personality and Social Psychology Bulletin* 31, no. 10 (2005): 1369–1385.

Johnson, M. A., R. M. Stevenson, and C. R. Letwin. "A Woman's Place Is in the…Startup! Crowdfunder Judgments, Implicit Bias, and the Stereotype Content Model." *Journal of Business Venturing* 33, no. 6 (2018): 813–831.

Kanze, D., L. Huang, M. A. Conley, and E. T. Higgins. "We Ask Men to Win and Women Not to Lose: Closing the Gender Gap in Startup Funding." *Academy of Management Journal* 61, no. 2 (2018): 586–614. https://doi.org/10.5465/amj.2016.1215

Lamont, M., L. Adler, B. Y. Park, and X. Xiang. "Bridging Cultural Sociology and Cognitive Psychology in Three Contemporary Research Programmes." *Nature Human Behaviour* 1, no. 12 (2017): 866–872.

Leitner, J. B., E. Hehman, O. Ayduk, and R. Mendoza-Denton. "Racial Bias Is Associated with Ingroup Death Rate for Blacks and Whites: Insights from Project Implicit." *Social Science & Medicine* 170, (2016): 220–227.

Madsen, S. R. and M. S. Andrade. "Unconscious Gender Bias: Implications for Women's Leadership Development." *Journal of Leadership Studies* 12, no. 1 (2018): 62–67.

Nosek, B. A., C. B. Hawkins, and R. S. Frazier. "Implicit Social Cognition: From Measures to Mechanisms." *Trends in Cognitive Sciences* 15, no. 4 (2011): 152–159.

Nosek, B. A., M. R. Banaji, and A. G. Greenwald. "Harvesting Implicit Group Attitudes and Beliefs from a Demonstration Web Site." *Group Dynamics: Theory, Research, and Practice* 6, no. 1 (2002): 101.

ODIHR (Office for Democratic Institutions and Human Rights). "Hate Crime Reporting 2018." *Hate Crime Reporting,* (2019). https://hatecrime.osce.org.

Orchard, J. and J. Price. "County-Level Racial Prejudice and the Black-White Gap in Infant Health Outcomes." *Social Science & Medicine* 181, (2017): 191–198.

Payne, B. K. and J. W. Hannay. "Implicit Bias Reflects Systemic Racism." *Trends in Cognitive Sciences* 25, no. 11 (2021): 927–936.

Payne, B. K., H. A. Vuletich, and K. B. Lundberg. "The Bias of Crowds: How Implicit Bias Bridges Personal and Systemic Prejudice." *Psychological Inquiry* 28, no. 4 (2017): 233–248.

Petty, R. E., R. H. Fazio, and P. Brinol. "The New Implicit Measures: An Overview." *Attitudes: Insights from the New Implicit Measures,* (2009): 3–18.

Pritlove, C., C. Juando-Prats, K. Ala-Leppilampi, and J. A. Parsons. "The Good, the Bad, and the Ugly of Implicit Bias." *The Lancet* 393, no. 10171 (2019): 502–504.

Rachman, G. "Nationalism Is a Side Effect of the Coronavirus." *Financial Times,* (2020). https://www.ft.com/content/644fd920-6cea-11ea-9bca-bf-503995cd6f

Rooth, D. O. "Automatic Associations and Discrimination in Hiring: Real World Evidence." *Labour Economics* 17, no. 3 (2010): 523–534.

Ross, H. J. *Everyday Bias: Identifying and Navigating Unconscious Judgments in Our Daily Lives.* Rowman & Littlefield, 2014.

Salles, A., M. Awad, L. Goldin, K. Krus, J. V. Lee, M. T. Schwabe, and C. K. Lai. "Estimating Implicit and Explicit Gender Bias among Health Care Professionals and Surgeons." *JAMA Network Open* 2, no. 7 (2019.

Schuman, H., C. Steeh, and L. Bobo. *Racial Attitudes in America: Trends and Interpretations* (Vol. 2). Harvard University Press, 1985.

Starck, J. G., T. Riddle, S., Sinclair, and N. Warikoo. "Teachers Are People Too: Examining the Racial Bias of Teachers Compared to Other American Adults." *Educational Researcher* 49, no. 4 (2020): 273–284.

Sukhera, J., C. J. Watling, and C. M. Gonzalez. "Implicit Bias in Health Professions: From Recognition to Transformation." *Academic Medicine* 95, no. 5 (2020): 717–723. doi:10.1097/ACM.0000000000003173

Tisdall, S. "Power, Equality, Nationalism: How the Pandemic Will Reshape the World." *The Observer,* (2020). https://www.theguardian.com/world/2020/mar/28/power-equality-nationalism-howthe-pandemic-will-reshape-theworld

Warikoo, N., S. Sinclair, J. Fei, and D. Jacoby-Senghor. "Examining Racial Bias in Education: A New Approach." *Educational Researcher* 45, no. 9 (2016): 508–514.

Zestcott, C. A., I. V. Blair, and J. Stone. "Examining the Presence, Consequences, and Reduction of Implicit Bias in Health Care: A Narrative Review." *Group Processes & Intergroup Relations* 19, no. 4 (2016): 528–542.

ABOUT THE AUTHOR

Dr. Zena Hamdan is a public health educator and scholar. She brings her diverse background and experience to practice through a well-thought-out approach to raise awareness and engagement to help people understand their challenges and needs to live a healthy, fulfilling, and rewarding lifestyle.